The Poodle

OUR BEST FRIENDS

OUR BEST FRIENDS

The Poodle

Janice Biniok

ELDORADO INK

Produced by OTTN Publishing, Stockton, New Jersey

Eldorado Ink
PO Box 100097
Pittsburgh, PA 15233
www.eldoradoink.com

First printing

1 3 5 7 9 8 6 4 2

Library of Congress Cataloging-in-Publication Data

Biniok, Janice.
  The poodle / Janice Biniok.
     p. cm. — (Our best friends)
  Includes bibliographical references and index.
  ISBN-13: 978-1-932904-24-6 (hc)
  ISBN-10: 1-932904-24-7 (hc)
  1. Poodles. I. Title.
  SF429.P85B56 2008
  636.72'8—dc22
                              2007044878

Photo credits: Courtesy National Association of Professional Pet Sitters, www.petsitters.org: 91;
© iStockphoto/Debi Bishop: 48, 84, front cover (left top and bottom); © iStockphoto/Kit Sen Chin:
29; © iStockphoto/Darinburt: 70; © iStockphoto/Jim Domke: 97; © iStockphoto/Lee Feldstein: 88;
© iStockphoto/Marianne Fitzgerald: 102 (right); © iStockphoto/Stacy Gamez: 18; © iStockphoto/
Gertjan Hooijer: 3; © iStockphoto/Eric Isselée: 20 (inset), 53 (dog), back cover; © iStockphoto/David
Kahn: 12 (top right), 22; © iStockphoto/Slobo Mitic: 33; © iStockphoto/Sylvia Nowik: 85; ©
iStockphoto/Oleg Prikhodko: 108; © iStockphoto/Monique Rodriguez: 81; © iStockphoto/
Ronibgood56: 59; © iStockphoto/Leigh Schindler: 19, 49; © iStockphoto/Duncan Walker: 20 (background); © iStockphoto/Yula Zubritsky: 74; © Jupiterimages Corporation: 41; © OTTN Publishing; 53
(worms); © Will Patch: 77; used under license from Shutterstock, Inc.: 8, 10, 12 (top left and
bottom), 13, 16, 23, 24, 25, 26, 28, 30, 31, 32, 35, 36, 37, 38, 40, 42, 44, 53 (mosquito and heart),
57, 61, 63, 64, 65, 66, 67, 69, 72, 75, 78, 79, 86, 92, 94, 95, 98, 100, 102 (left), 106, 107, 110, 111,
113, 115, 116, front cover (main, left center).

TABLE OF CONTENTS

Introduction

GARY KORSGAARD, DVM

The mutually beneficial relationship between humans and animals began long before the dawn of recorded history. Archaeologists believe that humans began to capture and tame wild goats, sheep, and pigs more than 9,000 years ago. These animals were then bred for specific purposes, such as providing humans with a reliable source of food or providing furs and hides that could be used for clothing or the construction of dwellings.

Other animals had been sought for companionship and assistance even earlier. The dog, believed to be the first animal domesticated, began living and working with Stone Age humans in Europe more than 14,000 years ago. Some archaeologists believe that wild dogs and humans were drawn together because both hunted the same prey. By taming and training dogs, humans became more effective hunters. Dogs, meanwhile, enjoyed the social contact with humans and benefited from greater access to food and warm shelter. Dogs soon became beloved pets as well as trusted workers. This can be seen from the many artifacts depicting dogs that have been found at ancient sites in Asia, Europe, North America, and the Middle East.

The earliest domestic cats appeared in the Middle East about 5,000 years ago. Small wild cats were probably first attracted to human settlements because plenty of rodents could be found wherever harvested grain was stored. Cats played a useful role in hunting and killing these pests, and it is likely that grateful humans rewarded them for this assistance. Over time, these small cats gave up some of their aggressive wild behaviors and began living among humans. Cats eventually became so popular in ancient Egypt that they were believed to possess magical powers. Cat statues were placed outside homes to ward off evil spirits, and mummified cats were included in royal tombs to accompany their owners into the afterlife.

Today, few people believe that cats have supernatural powers, but most pet owners feel a magical bond with their pets, whether they are dogs, cats, hamsters, rabbits, horses, or parrots. The lives of pets and their people become inextricably intertwined, providing strong emotional and physical rewards for both humans and animals. People of all ages can benefit from the loving companionship of a pet. Not surprisingly, then, pet ownership is widespread. Recent statistics indicate that about 60 percent of all households in the United States and Canada have at least one pet, while the figure is close to 50 percent of households in the United Kingdom. For millions of people, therefore, pets truly have become their "best friends."

Finding the best animal friend can be a challenge, however. Not only are there many types of domesticated pets, but each has specific needs, characteristics, and personality traits. Even within a category of pets, such as dogs, different breeds will flourish in different surroundings and with different treatment. For example, a German Shepherd may not be the right pet for a person living in a cramped urban apartment; that person might be better off caring for a smaller dog like a Toy Poodle or Shih Tzu, or perhaps a cat. On the other hand, an active person who loves the outdoors may prefer the companion-

ship of a Labrador Retriever to that of a small dog or a passive indoor pet like a goldfish or hamster.

The joys of pet ownership come with certain responsibilities. Bringing a pet into your home and your neighborhood obligates you to care for and train the pet properly. For example, a dog must be housebroken, taught to obey your commands, and trained to behave appropriately when he encounters other people or animals. Owners must also be mindful of their pet's particular nutritional and medical needs.

The purpose of the OUR BEST FRIENDS series is to provide a helpful and comprehensive introduction to pet ownership. Each book contains the basic information a prospective pet owner needs in order to choose the right pet for his or her situation and to care for that pet throughout the pet's lifetime. Training, socialization, proper nutrition, potential medical issues, and the legal responsibilities of pet ownership are thoroughly explained and discussed, and an abundance of expert tips and suggestions are offered. Whether it is a hamster, corn snake, guinea pig, or Labrador Retriever, the books in the OUR BEST FRIENDS series provide everything the reader needs to know about how to have a happy, well-adjusted, and well-behaved pet.

> Can such a classy-looking dog be a friendly family pet and companion? Absolutely! Poodles are among the most popular of all dog breeds.

CHAPTER ONE

Is a Poodle Right for You?

A favorite companion for royalty in France during the 18th century, a symbol of opulence in the United States during the Roaring Twenties, and blessed with an enduring reputation of elite elegance, the poodle does not appear to be a canine for commoners. And yet, there he is, one of the top ten most registered dog breeds with the American Kennel Club (AKC), and he has maintained this rank consistently for almost half a century.

What about the poodle is so extraordinary that it attracts so many people to the breed? If you were initially attracted to the poodle's trademark curly hair, you would not be the first to be curious about this unusual canine feature. If you fell in love with the poodle's snappy intelligence, joyful attitude, or loving personality, you are one of many who have been smitten by this dog's excellent character.

Besides having beauty and brains, the poodle is an amazingly versatile dog. The various sizes of poodle provide options for a large, sturdy playmate or a small, cuddly lapdog. His malleable appearance can range from powder puff to sport utility, depending on how he is groomed; this allows the poodle to fulfill any image his owner desires. The poodle's clean, nonshedding coat makes him very attractive as a house pet. And to give him just a little more of an edge over the competition, the poodle has a noble carriage that reflects his boundless self-confidence and self-esteem. With such an abundance of desirable qualities, it is no wonder the poodle appeals to people across a broad spectrum, regardless of age, gender, or social status.

CHOOSING THE RIGHT BREED

Even though the poodle fills many niches, this doesn't mean a poodle is a good match for every family and every situation. Daniel Tortora attempts to simplify the process of choosing a dog in his book *The Right Dog for You*. He writes, "The best choice, leading to the most satisfactory relationship between pet and caretaker, is the one that matches the personality and unique life-style of the owners with the temperamental characteristics of the breed." But in the poodle's case, this process must be taken a step further to encompass the physical characteristics of the

Young children can form strong bonds with Miniature Poodles, like the one shown here, or with the larger Standard Poodles.

dog, because the poodle's physical features reveal much about his needs.

Do you have what it takes to be a poodle owner? Does a poodle have what it takes to make you happy? You can only answer these questions by taking a closer look at the dog as a whole.

PHYSICAL CHARACTERISTICS

Not only do the physical characteristics of the poodle define the poodle's physical strengths and limitations, but they also signal the amount and type of care required to keep a poodle happy and healthy. Do these care requirements fit into your lifestyle? Are the poodle's physical traits consistent with the role you expect your dog to fill?

SIZE: Whether you want a hiking companion or a lap warmer, the poodle is one of the few breeds of dog that comes in three different sizes to meet various expectations. The largest, the Standard Poodle, tops the size chart at over 15 inches (38 cm) high at the peak of the shoulder, and generally weighs 50 pounds (23 kg) or more. Miniature Poodles stand over 10 inches (25 cm) and can reach up to 15 inches (38 cm) high. This middle-size poodle weighs between 12 and 18 pounds (5.5 and 8 kg). The most diminu-

tive, the Toy Poodle, does not exceed 10 inches (25 cm) in height and generally weighs between 6 and 9 pounds (3 and 4 kg).

Each of these sizes can be appropriate for different situations. Families with younger children should choose a Standard or Miniature Poodle that can keep up with the boisterous play of their children. Men may prefer the more substantial physique of the Standard variety, especially if they plan to take their dogs on outdoor adventures. On the other hand, people who travel frequently might do well with the eminently portable Toy Poodle.

STRUCTURE: Although the height and weight of each type of poodle is different, the poodle's physical form is the same whether it comes in a large package or a small one. The poodle is considered one breed, and, as such, all poodles must conform to

FAST FACT

Small dogs tend to have a greater life expectancy than their larger cousins, and this is also the case with poodles. Toy and Miniature Poodles are known to live 14 to 16 years, while Standard Poodles can expect to live 12 to 14 years.

POODLE CHARACTERISTICS

SIZE

Standard: over 15 inches (38 cm) at shoulder

Miniature: 10 to 15 inches (25.5 to 38 cm) at shoulder

Toy: under 10 inches (25.5 cm) at shoulder

COLORS

White, black, silver, gray, brown, cream, apricot, blue and café-au-lait

COAT

Curly, nonshed, requires daily brushing and clipping every six to eight weeks

ENERGY LEVEL

Moderate to very high

LEARNING RATE

Learns very quickly

LONGEVITY

Standard Poodles: 12 to 14 years

Toy and Miniature Poodles: 14 to 16 years

Standard Poodle

Miniature Poodle

Toy Poodle

the same physical characteristics, other than size. These characteristics include an athletic, tight construction of the muscles and skin. The poodle is built to be a natural acrobat, with sinewy legs and a graceful, lean body. His skin fits smoothly, without excess folds or wrinkles, and this gives the poodle a clean, sleek form beneath his wooly covering.

The ideal proportions of his body give the poodle superb balance and remarkable strength, which enable him to accomplish amazing feats of jumping, standing on fore or hind legs, or even performing flips. It's easy to see why the poodle was such a popular circus performer in bygone days!

COLOR: Along with a choice of sizes, another feature that adds spice to the options available to poodle owners is the breed's wide assortment of colors. Poodles come in nine official colors recognized by the AKC: white, black, brown, apricot, gray, silver, blue, cream, and café-au-lait (light brown). All these colors are required to be solid, according to AKC breed standards, but that hasn't deterred the efforts of a small group of breeders who seek to draw attention to parti-colored poodles. Parti-colored poodles possess two or more colors, usually in a patchy pattern, such as a white dog with black patches.

Typically, poodles come in a variety of solid colors, including apricot.

Colors, of course, are a matter of personal preference, but black and white are the most common, and therefore the most widely available. All these colors are presented in a kinky-curly coat that has its own special qualities, unique to this breed.

THE POODLE COAT: The poodle's lovely curly hair is perhaps the most dominant characteristic of the breed. It can radiate classy style in an endless assortment of fancy clips, or it can represent the dog's historical rugged hardiness with more modest grooming. In either case, the poodle does need to be groomed, and he needs to be groomed often.

Unlike other canine coat types, the poodle's coat does not reach a certain length and then stop growing. It grows and grows, and then grows some more. If the hair is not clipped occasionally, those perky ringlets will mat into unsightly globs that can cause significant discomfort for the dog.

Most poodle owners seek the services of a professional dog groomer to trim their dogs, but those with a little more creative ambition may choose to do it themselves. In either case, a poodle's coat should be trimmed every six to eight weeks to keep it manageable, and this involves a considerable investment in grooming services or grooming equipment. Are you up to this task?

On the bright side, there are some distinct advantages that make up for the high-maintenance grooming requirements of the poodle. The poodle's curly coat doesn't shed, as most other dogs' hair does. His coat tends to retain shed hair until it is brushed out, which makes the poodle an exceptionally clean household pet. Less shed hair means less household cleanup!

It also means less dander to infiltrate the home environment. Dander (the tiny flakes of skin and oils that cling to pet hair) is a worrisome trigger for allergies. The poodle's nonshed quality minimizes this allergen to the point where allergy sufferers with milder sensitivities can successfully share living quarters with a poodle without noticeable discomfort. For this reason, the poodle has

ARE POODLES HYPOALLERGENIC?

Poodles are often hailed as a hypoallergenic breed because their curly coats retain shed hair and dander, which are sources of allergic reactions in people. Although the poodle's nonshed characteristic is known to minimize allergic reactions, there really is no such thing as a truly hypoallergenic dog. Some hair and dander will still manage to infiltrate the environment and cause problems for people with sensitivities. Whether a poodle is a good candidate as a companion animal for someone with allergies depends on the person's sensitivity level and what other precautions are used to prevent flare-ups, such as medications, hygiene practices, and housecleaning regimens.

become one of the most popular canine companions for people with allergies to dogs.

TEMPERAMENT

The poodle's touchable, fuzzy exterior is indeed an attention grabber, but what about his personality? Here, too, the poodle has many qualities that have contributed to his widespread popularity. But along with the advantages presented by the poodle's temperamental traits, the poodle has emotional and intellectual needs that must be met.

INTELLIGENCE: If the poodle's fluffy coat is his most prominent physical characteristic, his extraordinary intelligence is his most outstanding personality trait. Poodles are listed as the second most intelligent breed of dog in Stanley Coren's book *The Intelligence of Dogs*, and this is obvious to anyone who has had the pleasure of training or observing a poodle.

Poodles are quick learners and they are quite adept at figuring things out for themselves. Dogs with a strong sense of deductive logic can sometimes get into mischief, and poodle owners may find it a challenge to keep a step ahead of their canine geniuses. Regular training is a positive way for these smart dogs to expend their prodigious mental energy.

FAST FACT

Standard and Miniature Poodles are among the top 10 best prospects as barking watchdogs, according to Stanley Coren's *Intelligence of Dogs*. Although the protective nature of poodles is moderate compared to other breeds, they do enjoy alerting their owners to anything happening in the immediate environment. In some cases, the poodle's enjoyment of barking may require you to train the dog to cease such noisemaking on command.

One of the most charming and delightful ways to mentally exercise a poodle is to teach him tricks. Poodles have both the physical endowments and the intellectual capacities to learn complex sequences of behavior. How would you like a dog that can pick up his own toys? It behooves a poodle owner to take advantage of the poodle's talents, either by putting the dog to useful work or by enjoying the poodle's gifts as an entertainer. The poodle's extraordinary intelligence, combined with a strong will to please, makes the poodle one of the most trainable dogs in the world.

SENSITIVITY: Scientists have traditionally believed that dogs do not experience emotions, but anyone who has owned a poodle is thoroughly convinced that the inner essence of the poodle is pure joy. Poodles have a zest for life that is often expressed in their "smiles," a canine expression of drawn-back lips that uplift at the corners, similar to a human smile. Such a positive attitude makes the poodle fun to play with, work with, and live with. To add to this happy demeanor, poodles have a delightful sense of humor that is often displayed through clownish antics. Poodles are natural performers and

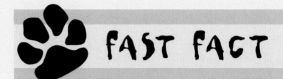

FAST FACT

You can't hide your feelings from a poodle. Poodles are extremely perceptive about human emotions. They notice very subtle differences in voice tone and body language.

thrive on the attention such behavior wins for them.

Poodles have also been credited with being amazingly perceptive about human emotions, which is one of the reasons they make excellent candidates for therapy dog work. But such a high degree of sensitivity requires gentle handling. Poodles can be easily stressed by heavy-handed training techniques or emotional upheaval in the household. If you treat your poodle gently and respectfully, you will have an emotionally balanced, contented dog—a fine animal companion.

FRIENDLINESS: Poodles are friendly dogs, although they can be somewhat cautious around strangers. Deep down, they truly enjoy giving love as much as they enjoy getting love, so any apprehension of strangers is quickly overcome by offering them sweet words and gentle petting. Poodles do not skimp on

Poodle owners are fond of the breed's fun-loving attitude and "smiling" appearance.

doggy kisses and attention for those they love. While their affectionate displays may seem annoying to some, others wholeheartedly welcome them.

THE BEST ENVIRONMENT FOR A POODLE

So the poodle is a sensitive, intelligent canine in a curly suit, but what do his characteristics really tell us about his needs? All dogs have basic needs that must be met to keep them happy and healthy, but these needs must be met in different degrees, depending on the breed of dog.

EXERCISE REQUIREMENTS: The poodle's athletic build is a clue to his physical activity needs. Not content to lie on the couch all day, poodles are considered active dogs that thrive on physical activity and the human attention that goes with it. A poodle's daily schedule should include a good aerobic workout of fetching, tugging, or playing for 20 to 30 minutes each day.

Toy and Miniature Poodles can often receive adequate exercise within the confines of their own homes, but Standard Poodles, due to their size, do require more room to romp. Because of this, Toy and Miniature Poodles can easily be kept in apartments while Standard Poodles would

prefer a yard. Even so, *all* poodles, regardless of their size, should be able to enjoy playtime and walks outdoors as part of their daily routine. Nothing beats the opportunities for socialization and new experiences that this provides. Dogs kept isolated in a home cannot develop the social skills they need to get along with other dogs or people, and they can easily become fearful or aggressive.

LIVING ACCOMMODATIONS: As important as outside experiences are for poodles, these dogs are not designed to spend *all* their time outside. The poodle's thick, wooly coat may appear to make him suitable to live in just about any type of climate—his coat can be shorn or left

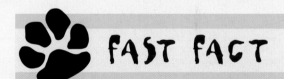

FAST FACT

As active dogs, poodles can sometimes present challenges for their owners. If a poodle's physical activity needs are not met, the intelligent poodle can think of some pretty ingenious—and often terribly undesirable—ways to expend his energy. The easiest way to avoid such problems is to provide regular exercise at the same time each day. When a poodle can count on a daily exercise session, he'll find it much easier to suppress his energy during the rest of the day.

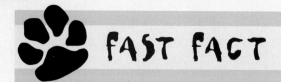

FAST FACT

The poodle was the most popular dog in the United States from 1960 to 1983, according to AKC registration statistics. No other breed of dog has yet surpassed this 23-year record.

long to tolerate extremes in temperature—but he would be woefully unhappy living an outdoor-only life.

It could be said that poodles are addicted to human attention and companionship; they are not emotionally equipped to live apart from their human families. Their attachment to humans is so strong that they are sometimes described as "needy" or "dependent." These dogs make excellent companions for people who want a pet that lives to be with his master. However, such devotion does come with a price—time and attention.

TIME AND ATTENTION: Poodles don't ask for attention: they *demand* it. This can seem burdensome for

Poodles thrive on interacting with humans. Always make time for your dog and make sure he receives the proper amount of mental and physical stimulation.

someone who doesn't have much time to devote to a dog, but poodles have a way of wiggling their way into people's hearts and inspiring them to make the time. They are the perfect dogs for people who like to include their canine companions in a variety of human activities, like going to the park, shopping, camping, or traveling.

Attention is a two-way street: Poodles demand a lot of attention, and they also give a lot of attention. Poodles are very attentive to their human caregivers, and this contributes to the extremely strong bond they develop with their owners. If you like a dog that seems capable of reading your mind, a poodle may be right for you. If you want a dog that is interested in and wants to be included in everything you do, a poodle may be your next best buddy.

Poodles just love to be with their owners, no matter what the activity may be. If you're an "always-on-the-go" type, expect your dog to want to come along on daily errands. This can become a good way to bond with your dog, as well as an opportunity for him to socialize with the world around him.

No matter what initially attracted you to poodles, you must take a close look at the breed to determine if a poodle should be in your future. After considering all the poodle's characteristics, both physical and temperamental, you might just find that you have fallen more deeply in love with the elegant and complex creature that originally caught your eye. If you allow yourself to become the center of a poodle's world, you'll discover that a poodle has become the center of yours!

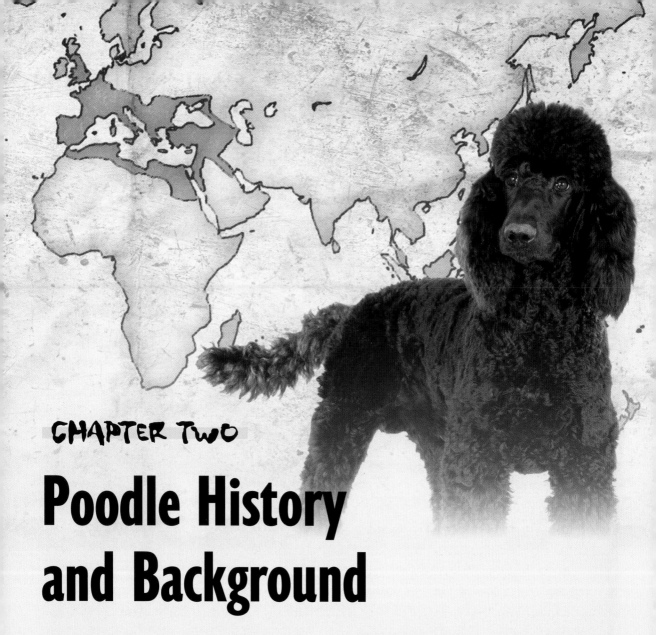

CHAPTER TWO

Poodle History and Background

The poodle's characteristics were developed through a long and interesting history, and it is both enlightening and helpful to study the breed's beginnings. How did the breed evolve into three different sizes? Why is the poodle's fur clipped in seemingly bizarre patterns? What can the poodle's history reveal about this breed's personality, talents and predispositions? Learning where the poodle came from is the same as taking a glimpse deep inside the poodle's soul. But there are always speed

The poodle breed originated in the Mediterranean region.

bumps and detours along the path of historical research.

BREED HISTORY

When it comes to breed histories, the problem most often encountered is the convolution of genetic lineage. This is because, up until the fairly recent establishment of breed clubs and registries in the late 1800s, crossbreeding was not only common—it flourished unabated. When breed club standards were created, only dogs that exhibited appropriate, uniform characteristics could be registered as members of a particular breed. Registries have since been closed in order to preserve the "purity" of canine lineage; only the offspring of registered dogs can now be registered as purebreds.

As Stephen Budiansky explains in his book *The Truth About Dogs*, "The . . . founding populations of nearly all breeds, including those with a long recorded history, were genetically diverse, and were not descended from any one exclusive population of ancient dogs or wolves."

This explains why there were different types of poodles recorded in early literature on the breed and why European artwork of the 15th and 16th centuries depicts poodles that have only a vague similarity to the poodle we know today. The single

characteristic all of the poodle's ancestors seem to have in common is the poodle's signature curly hair.

THE ANCIENT POODLE

It's impossible to know exactly when or where the mutation for curly hair occurred in dogs, but artifacts from A.D. 30 suggest that curly-haired hunting dogs existed at least as far back as ancient Roman times. Because the Roman Empire completely encircled the Mediterranean Sea by A.D. 150, it encompassed Arab, African, Asian, and European countries—the perfect environment for the amalgamation of races, cultures, and even dogs. So it's not surprising that the forebears of modern poodles have been historically linked to countries all around the Mediterranean Sea.

Some historians speculate that the poodle descended from the North African Barbet, a curly-haired dog reportedly imported to the Iberian Peninsula by the Arabs. This particular poodle ancestor may have given rise to the development of the Portuguese Water Dog, which in turn could have contributed to the later development of the Kerry Blue Terrier and the Irish Water Spaniel, both of Ireland. The Kerry Blue Terrier may be related to the less curly, more fluffy soft coated

Wheaten Terrier of Ireland and the lamb-like Bedlington Terrier of England. Add in all the other genetic crosses that went into creating these breeds, and it becomes obvious that the gene for curly hair was thrown into a vast melting pot of canine genes.

Through wars, conquests, droughts, and other conditions that spurred the migration of humans, dogs traveled extensive distances with their masters and spread their genetic material along the way. A single curly-haired dog could have passed on the gene for curly hair to many different

breeds in many different places. This might also explain why there are such varying degrees of curls, waves, and fluff within the canine gene pool. We now have hunting dogs with curly hair, terriers with curly hair, herding dogs with curly hair, protection dogs with curly hair, and small companion dogs with curly hair.

Poodles have traditionally followed a hunting heritage that may have begun with the ancient Roman hunting dogs; they still maintain a reputation as exceptionally efficient water retrievers. The smaller versions of poodle were not developed until

Although today the poodle isn't typically known for its proficiency in hunting, it is in fact a very capable and efficient water retriever.

much later, when dogs became valued for their companionship as well as their working ability.

THE POODLE IN GERMANY

The hunting poodle had become quite popular in Germany by the 16th century, as the poodle seemed perfectly suited to working and retrieving in marshlands. The poodle's kinky coat efficiently repelled water, and it also provided protective insulation against the cold, wet environment in which the dog worked. This may have been the point in history when specialized poodle clips emerged as a way to protect the dog against such harsh working conditions and to aid in the dog's mobility.

The fancy clips poodles now sport in the show ring are actually vestiges of this hunting heritage. The legs were shaved to reduce resistance, except for balls of hair left on knees and hocks to protect the joints. The poodle's chest was left with a thick mane to provide warmth for vital organs, and balls of fur were also left to protect the hip joints. These clips today are obviously greatly exaggerated, but there was a time when they served a useful purpose.

The poodle had become so popular in Germany that its name is derived from the German word *Pudel*, which means "water dog."

The poodle's unusual grooming style actually comes from its heritage as a hunting dog. Thicker areas of fur were left on the dog to keep important organs or joints warm while working in cold environments, while the rest was shaved away to help aid movement.

Even though the poodle later became more closely associated with France, most historians now agree that the poodle was originally a German breed. The medium-to-large-size German poodles still possessed

FAST FACT

The poodle was originally a medium-sized hunting dog, renowned for his skill in working in water. The smaller, lapdog versions of poodle were developed much later, possibly the result of cross-breeding with the Maltese.

varying physical characteristics, because at that time dogs were bred more for function and ability than for uniform physical characteristics. But the popularity of the poodle had ensured its continued success as a companion to humankind.

THE POODLE IN FRANCE

The poodle's hunting talents impressed the French, too, and the poodle became one of their favorite hunting companions. Called the *caniche* by French duck hunters, the larger hunting poodle was highly prized, but it was the smaller version of poodle that subsequently gripped the French so strongly that the poodle became the national dog of France.

It's impossible to know which breeds of dog were crossed with the larger hunting poodles to eventually produce the Toy and Miniature Poodles we know today. It's also beyond speculation to determine

where, exactly, small poodles originated. But what is certain is that the French embraced small poodles so wholeheartedly that Toy and Miniature Poodles are still commonly referred to as French Poodles.

Small poodles—there was no distinction between Toy and Miniature sizes at the time—became the darlings of anyone privileged enough to be able to afford a house pet. Being kept as companions for the nobility further bolstered the poodle's cachet, and this also prompted a change in the poodle's reputation: no longer

In France, small poodles became prized as companion pets.

Because of their compact size, Miniature Poodles make great pets for people who live in urban areas.

considered a rugged hunting dog, the poodle became the epitome of the pampered lapdog.

Miniaturized poodles were not large enough to use for hunting, but as companions their wonderful personality traits came to the fore, making them one of the most popular breeds of dog in the world. Their intelligence, happy disposition, and close emotional attachment to humans endeared them quite passionately to the French, but poodles were a treasure the French could not keep to themselves.

THE POODLE IN EUROPE

The poodle had one particular talent that may have contributed greatly to its dispersion throughout Europe—its talent as a performer. Traveling circuses and dog troupes employed both large and small poodles throughout the 1800s, and these public performances were a wonderful source of publicity for the breed. The poodle's unique, fuzzy exterior was groomed in ridiculously fancy fashions, which gained an enormous amount of attention. The poodle's incredible intelligence allowed him to learn complex routines, and his athletic abilities stunned spectators with acrobatic flips and lightning-fast spins.

The poodle had caught the eye of circus-goers throughout Europe, and by the late 1800s the poodle had already earned a reputation as an incredibly smart, agile, and talented canine. The first breed registry emerged at this time with the formation of the Kennel Club (KC) in Great Britain in 1873. The poodle quickly joined the ranks of registered dogs in 1874, and the Curly Poodle Club of England was established in 1876. Large and small poodles were all considered to be one breed, as they are today, but smaller poodles competed in the same class as larger poodles until 1910.

THE POODLE IN THE UNITED STATES

The European idea of breed registries and breed clubs for dogs was infectious, and the United States, which was strongly influenced by British trends during the 19th century, established the American Kennel Club (AKC) in 1884. It took the poodle considerably longer to wag its way into the hearts of Americans, however. Even though the first poodle was

Because of their ability to learn tricks and their remarkable physical agility, poodles were part of circus acts that traveled throughout Europe during the 19th century.

FAST FACT

The AKC is the largest purebred dog registry in the world, currently registering over 1 million dogs per year.

UNOFFICIAL SIZES

Breed standards are very specific concerning the size classifications for Standard, Miniature, and Toy Poodles. The Standard Poodle is any Poodle over 15 inches (38 cm) in height at the withers, which is the highest point of the shoulders. The Miniature Poodle stands over 10 inches (25.5 cm) and up to 15 inches (38 cm) at the withers, and the Toy Poodle is 10 inches tall (25.5 cm) or shorter.

Occasionally, Toy Poodles are advertised as "Tinies," or "Teacup" size, but these are not official size classifications. They are words that describe exceptionally small Toy Poodles. Even though the poodle breed standard does not disqualify these abnormally small poodles from the show ring, they have been known to suffer from an extensive list of genetic defects, and therefore are best avoided when purchasing a poodle.

registered with the AKC in 1887, the first American poodle club struggled to gain a pawhold on the west side of the Atlantic. Originally founded in 1896, the Poodle Club of America could not generate enough support to sustain itself and it was soon dissolved.

The lack of interest in poodles almost caused the breed to become extinct in the United States by the 1920s. Finally, more than three decades after its initial formation, the Poodle Club of America reemerged in 1931 to give American poodle fanciers the guidance and support of an official American breed club.

Since then, the poodle has earned the top honor of Best in Show

numerous times at America's premier dog show, Westminster. The Standard Poodle achieved this award in 1931, when Nunsoe Duc de la Terrace of Blakeen, an imported white poodle, made a strong impression. This finally gave the poodle a solid position among American dog fanciers. The Miniature Poodle achieved the Best in Show rank in 1943 with the win of Pitter Patter of Piperscroft. The Toy Poodle, whose petite size was not classified separately from Miniature Poodles until after 1940, finally gained a Westminster Best in Show award in 1956 through the charms of Wilbur White Swan.

Shortly after the Toy Poodle's success at Westminster, the poodle experienced a wild surge in popularity in the United States. Its numbers rose dramatically during the late 1950s to make it the most coveted dog in America by 1960, according to AKC registration statistics. Impressed by the poodle's elegant appearance, sparkling intelligence, and delightful joie de vivre, Americans clamored to possess these wonderful dogs, oblivious to the detrimental effects such popularity would have on the breed.

Irresponsible breeders, whose only goal was to profit from the huge demand for poodles, generated a host of genetic defects in poodles, ranging from eye problems to personality disorders. Fortunately, the poodle population boom stabilized and the frequency of genetic defects abated. It still took over two decades for the poodle to diminish somewhat in popularity. Today, the poodle remains one of the top ten most registered dogs in the United States.

BREED STANDARDS AND CONFORMATION

As mentioned earlier, it wasn't until the establishment of breed clubs in the late 1800s that formal breed standards were developed. A breed standard is a description of physical traits and temperament considered ideal for a particular breed of dog. Having common guidelines that describe the appearance and personality of poodles is a great help to breeders, who want to produce the best dogs possible. Breed standards also contribute to uniformity within the poodle breed so that poodles will

Breed standards were developed to distinguish unique characteristics that separate the poodle from other breeds.

FAST FACT

A renewed interest in the poodle's ability as a hunter led to the acceptance of Standard Poodles in AKC retrieving trials in 1998.

THE POODLE TAIL

There is one cosmetic adaptation to which all purebred poodles are subject, and that is the docking of their tails. A poodle's tail is customarily amputated to about half the tail's normal length when the poodle is only a few days old. The procedure, preferably performed by a licensed veterinarian, is quick, and the discomfort is minimal for puppies of this age.

all look alike without resembling other curly-haired dogs.

Poodle breed standards adopted by the Curly Poodle Club of England and the Poodle Club of America are very similar. Since the Standard Poodle, the Miniature Poodle, and the Toy Poodle are all considered one breed, they are expected to conform to the same requirements for physical Conformation. Anyone who studies the poodle breed standard will be armed with valuable knowledge that can help in choosing a poodle, even if the dog is only intended as a household companion.

Although it may be impossible to find a poodle that perfectly conforms to the archetype described in the poodle breed standard, poodles that come the closest to meeting these requirements earn top prizes at Conformation dog shows. Poor

Conformation, aside from being an indication of poor breeding, is a source of physical problems that can lead to exorbitant medical costs and devastating heartaches.

🐾 🐾 🐾

From hunting dog to house pet, the poodle has proven to be an exceptionally adaptable dog. He has waded through marshlands and sat before the thrones of kings. He has entertained us as a performer and befriended us as a loyal companion. More recently, he has comforted us as a therapy dog or helped us conduct searches and rescues. But regardless of the job he has done for us, it is the poodle's devotion to and love of humans that has earned him our enduring affection and admiration.

CHAPTER THREE

Responsible Pet Ownership

Did you know that when you bring a puppy into your life, your status in society changes? Your friends and relatives, your neighbors, members of your commu-nity, and even law enforcement per-sonnel look at you in a different way. You have entered the world of "dog ownership," where you are now responsible for a dog. Responsible

---

A poodle owner should make certain that her dog cannot escape the yard. A picket fence won't do; a fence at least six feet high is required for Standard Poodles.

pet ownership has become so important that both the American Kennel Club and the Kennel Club of the United Kingdom have extended the scope of their work in this area beyond purebred dogs to promote responsible dog ownership for all dog owners.

The AKC developed the Canine Good Citizen Test in 1989 to encourage dog owners to teach their dogs good manners. The KC implemented a similar test, called the Good Citizen Dog Scheme, in 1992. The AKC has recently gone a step further by encouraging organizations and communities to establish and celebrate a Responsible Dog Ownership Day by planning various dog-related events to draw attention to the campaign for responsible dog ownership.

So how do you become a responsible dog owner? Besides providing your poodle with adequate health care, nutrition, socialization, and training, as described in this book, you need to put safeguards in place to protect both your dog and the public. You need to make responsible decisions concerning neutering or spaying your dog. And you need to know what your legal responsibilities

are concerning dog ownership, and abide by the laws of your community.

IDENTIFICATION

One of the best safeguards you can provide for your dog is a form of identification so that he can be returned to you if he is ever lost or stolen. Most experts advise using two forms of identification—a collar with an ID tag, along with a permanent form of ID, such as a microchip or tattoo—for added protection.

An ID tag is the first type of identification most people will look for if they find a lost dog. The only problem with this form of ID is that collars can be lost or deliberately removed. This is why a permanent form of ID provides a good backup.

The most popular permanent form of ID is the microchip, an amazing technological gadget that is no larger than a grain of rice. The

It's a good idea to get a collar with sturdy fasteners to ensure that it doesn't fall off your dog.

FAST FACT

Some sources estimate that 1.5 million to 2 million dogs and cats are stolen in the United States each year. So being able to identify your poodle—through an ID tag, a microchip, or some other form of ID—is crucial.

microchip is injected under the skin between the dog's shoulders and remains there for the dog's lifetime. When a scanner is held over the dog, it reads the number on the microchip, which can then be traced to the dog's owner.

Tattoos have fallen out of favor somewhat since the advent of microchips, but they still have their proponents. Unlike microchips, tattoos are a visible form of permanent ID. Their application is virtually painless to the dogs, and they are usually placed on the inside of a rear leg or under the earflap where the dog's hair doesn't cover them so easily. Tattoo services keep a record of the tattoo number so that the dog's owner can be traced. One drawback of tattoos is that many people don't know where to look for them, so they may not be as

effective as microchips. Another drawback is that as the dog grows, the tattoo can stretch and fade, making it unreadable.

LICENSING

Most communities have laws requiring the licensing of dogs, and it's your duty as a responsible dog owner to comply with these laws. Licensing is a way for officials to keep track of the dogs that live in a community, make sure the dogs have been vaccinated against rabies, and return stray dogs to their owners. Not only do these laws make your community safer, they also help to protect your poodle.

You can probably look up your town's requirements for dog licenses online. Most municipalities have Web sites outlining license procedures and requirements.

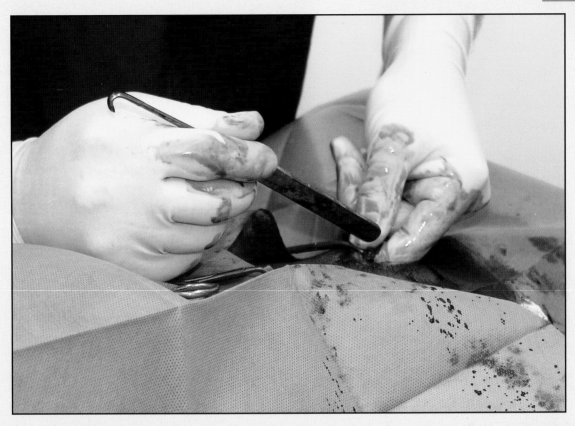

Choosing whether or not to spay or neuter your dog is an important decision. On one hand, there are many benefits, but on the other, scientific studies have found that there are some health-related side effects to having the procedure done.

will have to discourage robust activity for at least a week to prevent complications.

NEUTERING: Neutering has similar health benefits for male dogs, because it greatly reduces or eliminates the risk of prostate cancer, perineal hernia, or tumors of the reproductive organs. During this procedure, called castration, both testicles are surgically removed. This is much less invasive than spay surgery, so male dogs tend to recover more quickly than females.

Neutering and spaying are both conducted while a dog is anesthetized, so your dog will experience no discomfort during either procedure. Veterinarians have become more sensitive to the pain relief requirements of animals over the last decade, so your vet may prescribe some post-surgical pain medication, but these should only be used for a day or two. Pain is sometimes necessary to encourage a dog to take it easy after surgery, and Poodles, not known to let a little discomfort keep them down, may need this encouragement a little more than others!

KEEPING YOUR POODLE INTACT

If you plan to show or breed your dog, you will need to leave him intact, but you will also need to be prepared to manage sexually motivated behaviors and take the precautions necessary to keep your dog safe and to prevent accidental pregnancies. These are huge responsibilities that should not be taken lightly. In addition, you need to realize that the prospect of having a litter of adorably cute and playful poodle puppies is more appealing in concept than in reality.

Puppies can be messy, smelly, and noisy. They demand a lot of time and attention. The costs of puppy food, veterinary care, and supplies often turn out to be quite a bit higher than first-time dog breeders expect. And as a responsible breeder, you will need to take a strong interest in the welfare of the puppies your poodles produce and make sure they go to good homes. Unless you are willing to do everything necessary to give a litter of puppies the best start in life, you should leave the business of breeding to those who are seriously committed.

LEGAL ISSUES

Just as you establish household rules so that you can live harmoniously with your dog in a human

PET INSURANCE

Pet insurance policies can help cover health care expenses if your poodle develops a serious medical problem. Most pet insurance plans cover major illnesses and injuries. Every pet insurance plan is different, however, so research and compare several plans before making any final decisions.

Specific things to consider include the annual cost, the level of coverage offered, and any copays or deductibles. Every policy has exclusions, so you should also find out what is *not* covered. For example, many plans will not pay for preexisting conditions or elective procedures, like teeth cleaning. A final factor worth considering is whether the insurance company will pay your veterinarian directly, or will require you to pay bills, then submit a claim form to get reimbursed later.

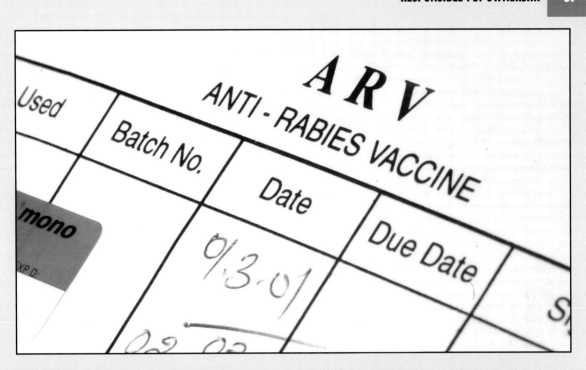

Federal and state laws require dogs to be vaccinated against rabies.

household, local and federal governments establish laws so that your dog can live harmoniously in the community. Laws that pertain strictly to pet ownership are designed to promote safety for both humans and animals, and to address conflicts that often arise between the two species.

SAFETY LAWS

Thanks to strict state requirements for rabies vaccinations for all dogs, rabies transmission from dogs to humans in the United States is now almost nonexistent. Unfortunately, this horrific and lethal virus still permeates the wild animal population,

so it is crucial to have your dog vaccinated against it. Make sure you know what the rabies vaccination requirements are in your state. Most states require a three-year booster vaccination, while others require an annual booster.

Be aware of any laws in your community relating to dog ownership. Some communities have a limit as to how many dogs you may keep on your premises. This helps to minimize nuisance complaints and guards against animal hoarding situations. Your community may also have a leash law that requires your dog to be on a leash any time he is off your property. This law is intended to encourage dog owners to keep their dogs under control at all times.

Dogs that are not under the control of their owners can wreak all kinds of havoc, causing property damage, injuries, and even deaths. Under general liability laws, you are responsible for the actions of your poodle, whether those actions occur on or off your premises. And considering the current litigious climate in our society, this is the best reason to teach your poodle good manners. Any problems with aggression, in particular, should be addressed with the help of a professional trainer.

BE A GOOD NEIGHBOR

General nuisance laws in your community may or may not have a provision addressing dog ownership in particular, but dogs that bark incessantly, whether indoors or out, are considered a nuisance. Don't leave

Be respectful of your neighbors. Keeping your poodle from barking excessively is not only considerate, but also required by law in many communities.

your dog unattended outside to bark and disturb your neighbors. If your dog is an inveterate indoor barker, you should find ways to train him to eliminate this behavior.

In the interest of good neighborly relations, you should also be sure to clean up your dog's waste when you are out with your dog. And keep in mind that not everyone loves your dog as much as you do. Some people are afraid of dogs, some people are allergic to dogs, and some people just don't care for dogs. So don't let your poodle approach someone unless you know the pup will be well received.

❧ ❧ ❧

Responsible pet ownership helps to ensure the acceptance of dogs in our communities, so that we can continue to enjoy the benefits of canine companionship. When you are a responsible dog owner, you shape the image others have of dogs and where they fit in our society, making the world a better place for dogs and dog lovers alike.

CHAPTER FOUR

The Best Possible Beginning

The poodle is naturally endowed with the right characteristics to bring many wonderful things into your life, like fun, happiness, and companionship. Toy and Miniature Poodles are, after all, bred specifically to be companions, and even Standard Poodles, despite their hunt-ing heritage, have a very strong affinity for humans.

And yet, this doesn't mean that forging an idyllic future with a poodle will be easy. The best possible outcome for you and your dog still depends on the best possible begin-ning. You need to choose the right

When choosing a poodle, consider your family, lifestyle, and the size of your home. Doing research and making an informed choice will be best for everyone.

dog from the right source, and make the best choice in a health care provider for your dog. Every journey begins with a single step, but let's make sure it's a step in the right direction!

CHOOSING YOUR DOG

Poodles share many physical and temperamental characteristics, but they also possess many individual differences. Within every litter of adorable poodle puppies, there are pups that are more energetic than others. Some may be more assertive while others are more submissive. Some may be excellent show prospects while others are destined to be house pets.

The future goals you have for your dog will obviously influence your choice. For instance, if you want a future Agility champion, you should choose the puppy whose energy and drive is at the high end of the scale. If you're looking for a therapy dog prospect, opt for a dog or puppy that enjoys meeting new people and avoid the shy ones. And if you want a show dog, you should not consider anything less than the best-quality dog you can afford from the best-quality source.

Besides keeping your dog's role in mind, you should also consider other choices available to you. Do you want a male or female? Do you want a puppy or an adult? And once you've decided on exactly what you want, where can you find it?

MALE OR FEMALE

Choosing between a male and female poodle is strictly a personal preference, since either sex, when neutered or spayed, can make an excellent pet. Unlike some breeds that exhibit more masculine and feminine personality differences between the sexes, poodles are not so inclined. A male can be just as sweet as a female, and a female can be just as bold and perky as a male.

This decision does carry more weight, however, if you intend to show your poodle. Show dogs are left intact

Poodles make great companions, regardless of whether they are male or female.

Raising a puppy can be fun, but be sure to prepare your home for this curious new family member.

(able to reproduce), because the whole purpose of honoring the best specimens of a breed is to encourage the reproduction of their superior traits. In this case, you will have to be willing to accept the responsibilities of owning an intact dog.

These responsibilities are quite different for a stud dog than they are for a brood bitch. Besides the different sexually driven behaviors you will have to manage, breeding carries different responsibilities and liabilities you should consider. Offering stud services and raising a litter of puppies are two completely different endeavors. You should do plenty of research and weigh the differences carefully before you choose between a male and female.

PUPPY OR ADULT

Poodle puppies are sweet little balls of fun and fluff, and it's impossible not to be captivated by their teddy bear–like cuteness. There are many advantages to raising a puppy, but there are also instances when it may be preferable to choose an adult dog.

One of the advantages of puppy rearing is that you can control the puppy's environment and upbringing. Puppies are blank slates, just waiting for someone to raise and train them to be perfect pets. They are also extraordinarily fun to play with, and it is such a rewarding experience to watch them grow up. Unfortunately, they can also be messy, destructive, mischievous, and noisy. It takes a great deal of time and patience to raise a poodle puppy.

Poodle puppies are also more expensive to care for than adults. They require a considerable amount of veterinary care during their first year, including a series of vaccinations, wormings, and sterilization surgery (if you're not going to keep them intact). Puppies outgrow many things, like beds, crates, and collars, all of which eventually have to be replaced. Add the cost of these things to the cost of items that are damaged during the puppy's teething and housetraining stages, and the total might reach up to $1,000 or more the first year!

Adult poodles, on the other hand, have outgrown the teething stage and may already be housetrained. The cost of adopting an adult dog from a shelter or rescue organization is significantly less than buying a puppy from a breeder, and the price usually includes the necessary vaccinations and sterilization surgery. Occasionally, adult dogs can be obtained from breeders, who sell adult dogs at discounted prices to manage the population of their breeding programs.

FAST FACT

The Internet has become a popular way to locate the right dog. Adoptable poodles and puppies for sale can be located anywhere in the country, all via the information superhighway. But beware of purchasing a puppy online. You should never purchase a puppy without first seeing it in person and inspecting its living conditions.

These "secondhand dogs" do carry with them past experiences that may influence their behavior. You might shy away from having to break a dog of a previously learned bad habit, but the work that goes into retraining an adult dog is not necessarily more demanding than training a puppy. Poodles are amazingly adaptable, even as adults, so they have the potential to become great pets regardless of their age.

WHERE TO FIND A POODLE

Fortunately, it doesn't take a private detective to locate oodles of poodles, since the poodle is a very popular breed. However, it does take careful evaluation to make sure your poodle comes from a reputable source. Poodles from less than savory sources may exhibit temperament deficiencies, such as neurotic or aggressive behaviors, or genetic

PAPERS YOUR BREEDER SHOULD SUPPLY

American Kennel Club registration papers—These are necessary to register the dog or puppy in your name.

Puppy sale contract—Reputable breeders issue puppy sale contracts to help ensure the welfare of the puppies they sell. The advantages for puppy buyers is that these contracts help avoid misunderstandings by outlining the responsibilities of both the breeder and the buyer, and they note, in writing, any health guarantees.

Pedigree—This is a chart of the dog's or puppy's family tree. The availability of this information shows that the breeder is serious about keeping meticulous records of her breeding program.

Health records—These should document any veterinary care your dog or puppy has received, including vaccinations, wormings, medications and surgeries.

defects due to poor breeding practices. So it is very important to evaluate the source of a poodle and exercise the self-control necessary to walk away from a charming poodle whose provenance makes him undesirable.

FINDING A RESPONSIBLE BREEDER

Poodle breeders can be found through dog shows, newspaper ads, veterinarians, professional groomers, local poodle clubs, or poodle Web sites. Whether a breeder is interested in breeding poodles for show, for profit, or as pets,

there are signs that every poodle buyer should watch for.

First, check out the puppies' environment. Is it clean? Do the puppies have ample

When selecting your puppy from a breeder, he should appear happy and healthy, with bright eyes and a clean coat.

room to run around and play? Do they have toys to play with and chew on? Are they allowed outdoors for fresh air and a change of scenery? Is the mother dog present? All these conditions are necessary to give a young puppy a good start in life. Regardless of the quality of breeding, a puppy that is isolated, confined to a pitifully small space, or separated from its mother and littermates at too young an age may suffer irreversible damage to its social or physical development.

Second, look at the puppy's overall physical condition. Does the puppy appear to be healthy and clean? There should be no sign of runny eyes, nasal discharge, diarrhea, lethargy, flaky skin, dull coat, fleas, or the potbelly appearance that often indicates a worm infestation.

Third, evaluate the puppy's records. Is the puppy at least eight weeks old, and has he received at least one set of puppy vaccinations? If so, the breeder should have proof of vaccinations from her veterinarian. If the puppy can be registered with the AKC or another reputable registry, has the proper paperwork been filed? *Never* take a breeder's word that registration papers will be forthcoming. This is a very good indication that the proper paperwork has *not* been filed with the registry and the puppy may not be eligible for registration.

Is a pedigree, which documents the puppy's family tree, available? If so, take a careful look or ask someone who knows about breeding to examine the pedigree. Does it indicate excessive inbreeding by the overrepresentation of certain ancestors' names? A certain amount of inbreeding is an acceptable part of responsible breeding, but outcrossing to other lines of poodles is also necessary to prevent hereditary health problems.

ADOPTING A DOG

Another viable option is to adopt a poodle from an animal welfare organization. The Humane Society of the United States estimates that 25 percent of the dogs taken in by animal shelters are purebreds, and there are bound to be a few poodles

FAST FACT

Most animal welfare organizations require adopters to sign a contract. These adoption contracts are designed to protect the welfare of the animals and generally do not include unreasonable requests that go beyond what would normally be expected of a responsible pet owner.

among them. Still, it can be a challenge to locate a poodle from this source, since poodles seem to find new homes quickly.

The chances of finding an adoptable poodle to fit your needs, wants, and lifestyle are much greater if you contact a rescue organization that specializes in poodles. The Poodle Club of America publishes a list of poodle rescue groups on its Web site, www.poodleclubofamerica.org. Another great Internet resource for potential adopters is www.petfinder.com, which makes it easy to search for a specific dog breed within a particular geographic area. This site maintains the most extensive nationwide database of adoptable animals in the United States.

Adopting an adult poodle can be more affordable than purchasing a puppy, but there are other benefits to adoption as well. Animal shelters often test the temperament of their dogs to make sure they are suitable for a particular living situation. This helps eliminate the uncertainty about whether a dog will get along with the family cat or be an appropriate companion for children. Animal shelters can also offer invaluable support to new dog owners in the form of behavioral advice, training classes, and care seminars.

Poodle rescue organizations can offer even greater benefits. Since they specialize in poodles, they are an exceptional resource for information and advice on the breed. Most rescue organizations place their dogs in foster homes, rather than kennels, until they are adopted. This gives the organization much more insight into each dog's personality and behavior in a home environment, which is crucial information for prospective adopters. But whether you purchase your poodle from a breeder or adopt one from an animal shelter or rescue organization, it is still important to evaluate the puppy or dog in terms of health and suitability.

EVALUATING A DOG OR PUPPY

To gain insight into the unique personality of an individual poodle, your best bet is to ask someone who has already spent time with the dog or puppy. An observant breeder can quickly point out the pups in a litter that are more outgoing or more reserved. She will know which puppies have the greatest potential for Obedience competitions, showing, search-and-rescue, or therapy-dog work. Shelter adoption counselors and foster home volunteers, likewise, can give you valuable information about a particular poodle and tell you about his specific needs, quirks, and characteristics. In addition, you should conduct an evaluation of your own.

EVALUATING A PUPPY: Even though puppies tend to exhibit some of their personality traits at a young age, it's still difficult to determine exactly what a puppy will be like as an adult. When it comes to personality and behavior, puppies grow up to become products of both their genetics and their environments. The best indication of what to expect from your puppy's genetics can be acquired by observing your puppy's parents. If at least one parent is available—usually the mother—you can get a good idea if your puppy will grow up to be friendly, timid, excitable, or calm.

It's just as important to evaluate the parent dogs' physical characteristics to be sure you are getting a quality puppy. If you are looking for a show prospect, physical characteristics are a premium commodity that you should thoroughly research and doggedly pursue. If you seek a pet-quality poodle, a few physical flaws won't make any difference as long as your pooch of choice has an outgoing, friendly personality. And if you yearn for the exhilaration and excitement of raising a dog to become an athlete, abundant energy, intelligence, and a strong will to please are all traits that will serve you and your dog well.

EVALUATING AN ADULT DOG: Adult dogs are a little easier to evaluate because their personality traits are already fully developed. While all puppies have bursts of seemingly boundless energy, they don't all grow

DETERMINING YOUR PUPPY'S APTITUDE

The potential for a puppy to fill any specific role has been turned into something of a science. Jack and Wendy Volhard, well-respected dog trainers and authors, have devised the Puppy Aptitude Test to make it easier to evaluate puppies. The test, in its entirety, can be viewed on their Web site, www.volhard.com. Psychologist and canine intelligence expert Stanley Coren developed both a Canine IQ Test and an Obedience Personality Test, which are outlined in his book *The Intelligence of Dogs*. If you have specific goals for your poodle puppy, consider evaluating him using one or more of these methods.

Adopting an adult dog can be a rewarding experience. The dog has already gone through his puppyhood, therefore eliminating a lot of the hard work involved in raising a puppy.

up to have high energy levels as adults. All puppies have a natural instinct to chase or follow, but this doesn't mean they will all have a strong prey drive (the desire to chase moving things) as adults. And even though puppies learn to bend to the authority of adult dogs, as adults some will have submissive personalities while others won't. All these personality traits—energy level, prey drive, and dominance—can be directly and accurately observed in adult dogs.

Keep in mind, however, that you cannot change a dog's personality or temperament. Personality traits can be managed or controlled, but they cannot be eliminated altogether. A high-energy dog will always be a high-energy dog. A dog with a strong prey drive that loves to chase cats will always love chasing cats. A dominant dog will always be a dominant dog.

Behavior, however, can be modified with training. So don't let a few bad habits like begging, pulling on the leash, or jumping dissuade you from adopting an adult poodle. Most shelter dogs have received little or no training, and they are just waiting for someone to unlock their genius and good behavior!

CHOOSING A VETERINARIAN

Choosing a veterinarian is part of providing the best possible beginning for your dog because health care, as an investment in your dog's future, needs to start early. There are many horrible, but preventable, diseases that can cut your poodle's life short if you don't attend to your dog's health care from the very start.

There is nothing trivial about choosing a health care provider for a cherished canine companion, and your priority should be finding someone you can trust. You can ask for referrals from friends, relatives, or coworkers, but a better source may be your dog's breeder or a local poodle rescue group. They may be able to recommend a vet who has experience with the specific health needs of poodles.

In either case, it's important to choose a veterinarian or clinic within relatively close driving distance in case of a medical emergency. You can choose several clinics in close proximity to your home, and then conduct initial telephone interviews with each of them. Ask what they charge for office visits, vaccinations, and spay or neuter surgeries, so you can determine if they have competitive prices. Ask about the facility and equipment to find out if they have their own ultrasound and blood-testing equipment, or if they refer their clients to other facilities for these services. Do their hours of operation conflict with your work schedule? And where will you need to go for emergency services when the clinic is closed?

Once you narrow down your choices, make an appointment to meet each of the veterinarians in person without your poodle. Offer to pay for this time so you can make a good evaluation of each vet. Then,

Your poodle's first veterinary office visit is an important one. Your dog will be seeing this vet over the course of his lifetime, so it's important to choose his doctor carefully.

once you decide on your favorite, schedule your pup for a health checkup appointment.

You should take your newly acquired dog or puppy for a veterinary checkup shortly after purchase or adoption, even if he is up-to-date on his vaccinations. This will give you the peace of mind that your new pet does not have a serious health issue that you were unable to detect.

On your first visit, notice how the office staff and veterinarian treat you and your dog. It's not unusual to encounter longer waiting times on days when emergencies seem to outnumber appointments for routine care, but you should still be treated with courtesy and kindness. Are the exam rooms clean and well organized? Does the veterinarian take the time to answer your questions? Do you feel comfortable there? If you feel good about the facility, your dog probably will, too.

THE VETERINARY EXAM

When you take your puppy in for his first checkup, there are several things you should be sure to bring along. Jot down any questions or concerns you may have about your puppy's health or behavior so you can discuss them all at your appointment. Your vet will also ask you to bring in a stool sample from your puppy so it

can be checked for the presence of internal parasites. And be sure to bring along any information your breeder may have given you about your puppy's health. This includes vaccination records, documentation of any illnesses and treatments, and any pertinent health information regarding your puppy's parents. Your veterinarian will appreciate knowing your puppy's hereditary background as well as what kind of health care he has previously received.

At your puppy's first physical examination, your veterinarian will literally check out your puppy from head to toe. His eyes will be checked for potential vision problems; his ears will be checked for signs of deafness, infections, or mites; and his mouth will be checked for oral problems as well as signs of other diseases. His heart and lungs will be checked by stethoscope, and his abdomen will be palpated to detect any abnormalities.

FAST FACT

A female flea consumes 15 times her own weight in blood daily. It's easy to see how a severe infestation of fleas on a puppy, which has such a small body mass, can result in acute anemia or even death.

Your puppy's skin and coat will also be checked for fleas or other parasites.

EXTERNAL PARASITES

Fleas and ticks are extremely bothersome pests that like to live on the surface of your dog, where they bite the skin and consume blood. Fleas are notorious for reproducing at an incredible rate, and just a few fleas on your dog can quickly become a major infestation within a few weeks. Before you know it, they have set up housekeeping in your couches, beds, and carpeting, or any other place your dog spends time!

Flea bites cause itching and inflammation that can make your dog horribly uncomfortable. Even worse, when your dog becomes overburdened with fleas, these little critters will begin to target people! Fleas are also hosts for tapeworm larvae, which can easily be transmitted to your dog. Eradicating these pests involves treating your dog and your home with the appropriate pesticide products, recommended by your veterinarian. Then, a second treatment must be applied one to two weeks later to kill newly emerging fleas that were not destroyed with the first application.

Ticks do not cause nearly as much physical discomfort for dogs, but as blood-sucking pests, they are responsible for transmitting a number of

CANINE TICK-BORNE DISEASES

Lyme disease: Causes various degrees of joint swelling, arthritis, fevers, and fatigue.

Ehrlichiosis: Symptoms include anemia, high fever, and lethargy.

Tick paralysis: Characterized by a lack of coordination of the rear limbs, which may progress to complete paralysis of the rear legs.

Rocky Mountain spotted fever: Obviously causes a fever, but is also known to cause loss of appetite, vomiting, diarrhea, muscle and joint aches, anemia, and neurological symptoms, such as dizziness and seizures.

Babesiosis: Known to cause fever, anemia, weakness, depression, dehydration, and shock.

serious diseases, such as Lyme disease, ehrlichiosis, and Rocky Mountain spotted fever. Ticks burrow their heads into the dog's skin and can be difficult to remove. They are most often attracted to dogs' ears, heads, and necks, and the female tick can become quite large as her body gets engorged with blood.

If you find a tick on your dog, remove it by grasping the tick close to its head with tweezers and pulling it off using firm, steady pressure. Don't yank, or the tick's head may remain under the skin, where it can become infected. If you live in an area where ticks are abundant, you might want to consider using a flea and tick collar or a spot-on treatment to repel these pests.

INTERNAL PARASITES

Internal parasites may not cause as much apparent physical discomfort as external parasites, but the deleterious effect of these critters on your dog's health is tremendous nonetheless. Often referred to as worms, these parasites are detected when your veterinarian examines the stool sample you provide, or, in the case of heartworms, by doing a blood test.

Intestinal worms include roundworms, hookworms, whipworms,

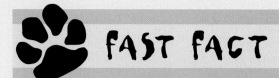

FAST FACT

Want a good reason why you should have your puppy tested and treated for worms? Almost all dogs are infected with roundworms at birth, and these parasites are easily transmitted to humans, according to the National Institutes of Health, U.S. Dept. of Health and Human Services.

and tapeworms. Although the housekeeping and husbandry habits of each one is different, they all sap vital energy from your dog and can seriously compromise his health. It is very common for puppies to acquire worms through their mother's blood supply while still in utero, or from their environment after they're born. That's why all puppies should be checked and treated for internal parasites. Your veterinarian can identify the particular parasite and prescribe the appropriate treatment.

Heartworms prefer to live in the circulatory system of dogs and grow to adulthood within the chambers of the heart. They are spread by mosquitoes, which serve as intermediate hosts in the process of their development. Heartworms can do significant damage to the heart and lungs, and treatment can be risky, depending on the severity of infestation. Due to the serious health consequences and difficulties in treating heartworms, it is highly recommended that you have your dog tested for heartworm and keep your dog on a heartworm preventative prescribed by your veterinarian. This is one parasite issue that is definitely easier to prevent than it is to cure.

VACCINATIONS

After your puppy receives a clean bill of health, he can receive any

THE DANGER OF HEARTWORMS

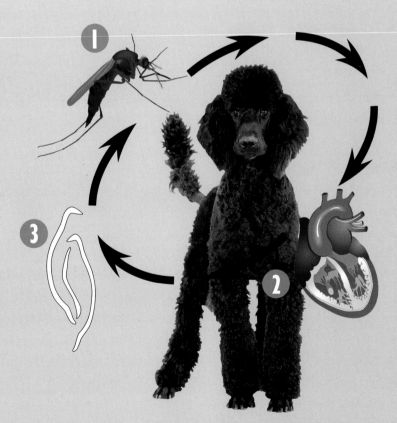

Heartworms are a concern for all dog owners. The graphic above illustrates the cycle of heartworm development. When a mosquito (1) bites a poodle, it can inject microfilaria into his bloodstream. The microfilaria travel through the bloodstream to the heart (2), where they grow into heartworms (3) and multiply, clogging the dog's heart. If left untreated, heartworms can kill.

VACCINATION SCHEDULE FOR PUPPIES

The following vaccination schedule is recommended by the American Animal Hospital Association:

Vaccine	Age of Puppy
Distemper	8 weeks and 12 weeks
Parvovirus	8 weeks, 12 weeks, 16 weeks
Parainfluenza	8 weeks, 12 weeks
Coronavirus	8 weeks, 12 weeks
Canine adenovirus-2	8 weeks, 12 weeks
Leptospirosis	8 weeks, 12 weeks
Bordetella*	12 weeks
Lyme disease*	12 weeks, 16 weeks
Rabies +	16 weeks

* Optional vaccines, depending on location and risk.   + Required by law.

Source: American Animal Hospital Association

vaccinations that he needs at this stage of his development. Vaccinations for a number of diseases are recommended for all dogs because of the high risk of transmission and the serious health consequences they represent. These include distemper, parvovirus, coronavirus, rabies, parainfluenza, canine adenovirus, and leptospirosis. Additional vaccines are available to protect against diseases that are not considered universal risks, such as bordetella and Lyme disease.

Most of these diseases are viral and there is no cure for them, which means treatment is limited to treating the symptoms with medications to alleviate vomiting and diarrhea, and providing supportive care in the form of intravenous fluids. Some of these diseases are very serious or even deadly for puppies, so it is crucial to have your puppy vaccinated according to the schedule recommended by the American Animal Hospital Association.

DISTEMPER: Distemper affects the nervous system and is fatal to 75 percent of infected puppies. Symptoms include eye and nasal discharge, severe listlessness, fever, vomiting and diarrhea.

PARVOVIRUS: Parvovirus is a highly contagious gastrointestinal virus that causes high fevers, vomiting, and bloody diarrhea. It can be fatal for puppies.

CORONAVIRUS: Coronavirus is another life-threatening, gastrointestinal disease that results in a loss of appetite, vomiting, and diarrhea.

RABIES: By far, the most frightening and deadly of all dog diseases is rabies. This virus attacks the nervous system and causes symptoms ranging from throat paralysis and the inability to swallow (which causes the drooling commonly described as "frothing at the mouth") to delirium and hyperaggressiveness. Due to the seriousness of this disease, and its risk of transmission to humans, state laws have been enacted to require the vaccination of all dogs against this disease. Be sure to check with your vet about your state's requirements concerning this vaccination.

PARAINFLUENZA: Parainfluenza is a respiratory virus that is generally not serious by itself, but which can reduce your puppy's immunity to secondary infections like pneumonia. Symptoms include coughing and nasal discharge.

CANINE ADENOVIRUS-2: Canine Adenovirus-2 is an upper respiratory infection that causes a hacking cough. Although this virus is considered mild, the vaccine for this disease provides protection against a much more serious virus called canine adenovirus-1, also known as infectious canine hepatitis. Canine adenovirus-1 causes the more serious consequences of jaundice and liver damage.

LEPTOSPIROSIS: Leptospirosis is a bacterial disease that can also damage the liver. Symptoms range from fever and jaundice to the excessive consumption of water.

BORDETELLA: Bordetella is a common, highly contagious bacterial infection of the respiratory system that causes chronic coughing. Also known as "kennel cough," this disease is not considered serious, but vaccination is recommended for dogs that come in contact with other dogs in a group setting, such as a kennel or dog show. This optional vaccine is administered through an intranasal spray.

LYME DISEASE: Lyme disease can cause fever, loss of appetite, arthritis, listlessness, and joint swelling. This vaccine is only recommended for dogs that live in areas where ticks are prevalent.

COMMON HEALTH PROBLEMS

Not only should you know how to prevent contagious diseases, but your puppy's future health also depends on your familiarity with, and your ability to recognize the symptoms of, genetic disorders. No matter what the quality of breeding that produced your puppy, all purebred dogs are susceptible to common hereditary defects.

Fortunately, new tests are being developed all the time to detect the presence of defective genes and assist breeders in eliminating genetic defects from their breeding programs. Some of the most common hereditary health conditions to which poodles are prone include eye problems, neurological disorders and orthopedic problems.

EYE DISORDERS: Poodles are highly susceptible to a number of hereditary eye conditions, one of which is cataracts. A cataract is an opaque spot on the lens of the eye that can grow to the point of causing total blindness. Treatment options should be discussed with a veterinarian, and depend on the severity and rate of progression of the condition. In severe cases, the lens of

the dog's eye will have to be replaced with an artificial lens.

Another eye condition, entropion, involves a defect that causes the eyelid of one or both eyes to roll inward and irritate the eye. This particular defect must be surgically treated in order to prevent scarring of the cornea, which can cause permanent vision loss. This condition is characterized by obvious discomfort in the eyes, tearing, squinting, and eye discharge.

Epiphora is another very common, but generally less serious, eye condition that involves excessive tear production. This condition is most noticeable with white or light-colored poodles, because the excess tears leave dark brown stains under the eyes. Some cases of epiphora in poodles require surgical intervention, while others simply require good hygiene to prevent the skin under the eyes from becoming irritated or infected.

The most devastating eye condition known to affect poodles is progressive retinal atrophy (PRA). This hereditary disease, which affects a number of dog breeds, progressively destroys the retina until total blindness results. A noticeable loss of vision without evidence of cataracts is a good indication that a poodle may have PRA.

NEUROLOGICAL DISORDERS: The neurological disorders that affect

Epiphora causes excessive tear production, which leaves discolored trails along the poodle's snout. If your poodle has symptoms like the one pictured above, contact your veterinarian to have him examined.

poodles can be somewhat perplexing to treat, but great strides have been made with the use of medications and diet to manage conditions like epilepsy and narcolepsy. Epileptic seizures can be quite disconcerting to witness: the dog will jerk and tremble uncontrollably during a fit, which can last from a few seconds to several minutes. A dog that experiences any type of seizure should receive veterinary attention immediately.

Narcoleptic seizures are altogether different. Dogs suffering from this type of seizure will collapse unexpect-edly into a deep sleep. This condition, too, can often be managed with medication to reduce the frequency of seizures, but it is not curable. In some cases, the frequency of seizures declines or abates on its own. Steps should be taken to keep an affected dog in safe areas where he cannot fall and injure himself if a seizure occurs.

ORTHOPEDIC DISORDERS: Orthopedic problems tend to be a common bane of both large and small poodles, although they appear in different forms. Toy and Miniature

Poodles are prone to medial patellar luxation, which can be described as a "trick" kneecap. This condition involves an unstable kneecap that slips out of its groove in the femur bone. It is very common among many small breeds of dog, and it causes pain and some dysfunction of the joint. Dogs with this condition will express different degrees of pain by limping, hopping, or skipping with their back legs, and the best treatment will be determined by the severity of the condition. Mild forms can be managed with pain medication and exercise restrictions, while severe cases can be treated successfully with surgery.

Standard Poodles are subject to an orthopedic problem more common in larger dogs: hip dysplasia. This condition is caused by a loose or improper fit of the ball-and-socket joint of the hip, which causes wear on the joint. Eventually, damage to the joint results in pain, lameness,

and osteoarthritis. Treatment often consists of pain management, anti-inflammatory drugs, joint supplements, and controlled exercise. In severe cases, total hip-replacement surgery may be necessary.

Early detection and treatment of hereditary conditions can often result in a better prognosis or better quality of life for your dog. The more you know about the health of your poodle, the better health care decisions you will be able to make. Your poodle relies on you to keep him "smiling!"

🙰 🙰 🙰

To be the best possible human companion for your new dog, you have to fulfill your responsibilities, from your first day together. A great beginning not only leads to a great future, it also makes the journey so much more enjoyable. So settle in with your poodle and enjoy the ride!

CHAPTER FIVE

Caring for Your Puppy (Birth to Six Months)

Introducing a poodle puppy into your household is sure to add joy, fun, and even a little bit of craziness to your life. It's natural to be excited about adding this new element to your life, and there is no better way to express your enthusiasm than by preparing for your puppy's arrival.

It will take time for your puppy to adjust to his new home. This transition will be easier for everyone if you prepare your home properly before he arrives.

Both you and your new puppy will need to adjust to a new life situation, and this means that along with the fun comes a bit of stress. Advance preparations can help make these adjustments go much more smoothly for both of you, and you can avoid some of the worry and look forward to more of the enjoyment. You need to think about where the puppy will sleep, where he will eat, and where he will be kept during the day when nobody is home.

LIVING ARRANGEMENTS

Your poodle puppy will prefer to sleep near his new human companions, so you might want to make arrangements to bed your puppy down in a comfortably padded crate next to your bed. Some puppies, however, miss their mother and littermates terribly for the first few days and may spend their nights expressing their loneliness in nerve-wrenching cries. There are some things you can do to remedy this situation.

First, make sure your puppy plays hard and has a potty break right before bedtime so that he will be tired enough to sleep. Then, put him to bed in his crate with a warm water bottle wrapped in a towel to simulate the close body contact he is used to having with his littermates at nighttime. If these techniques don't work, it's always a good idea to have a backup sleeping arrangement in mind. If you have to temporarily crate your puppy in a laundry room or bathroom at night so the human occupants in your home can get a good night's sleep, don't feel guilty. Your puppy should settle down in a few days so he can join you at nighttime.

Figuring out where your puppy will eat is a little simpler. There are just two things to keep in mind—flooring that is easy to clean and a place that is out of the way of traffic patterns. A corner of the kitchen or laundry room is a good choice. If you have other dogs or cats, choose a place that won't cause conflicts with the feeding of your other pets.

Then there is the problem of determining what to do with your puppy when no one is home to supervise him. For short absences of an hour or two, it won't hurt to keep your puppy in his crate, but this is too small a space to keep your puppy confined if you will be gone for longer periods. For proper physical growth and development, puppies need adequate room to move around during the day. A puppy pen or a small room is a much better option for longer lengths of confinement, but whatever area you choose, it should be puppy-proofed for safety.

In fact, any area of your home where your puppy will be allowed to roam, explore, and play should be checked for safety hazards. Poodle puppies are naturally curious and haven't yet learned to beware of dangerous situations. So check your home for exposed electrical cords, toxic houseplants, and any items within your puppy's reach that may become chewing or choking hazards. The best way to do this is to get down on your hands and knees so you can see things from your puppy's point of view. Toy Poodles are especially small and can wiggle into very tight places, so cover or block any openings to areas that might cause problems.

Your puppy will be curious about his new home and all the things in it.

FAST FACT

Poodle puppies love to explore with their mouths, by testing the taste, texture, and hardness of objects. Even though puppies learn a lot this way, they also expose themselves to many hazards with this behavior. Puppy-proof your home to prevent accidental electrocution, choking, or poisoning.

ESTABLISHING HOUSEHOLD RULES AND RESPONSIBILITIES

Deciding which areas of your home your puppy will have access to is just one of the household rules you should establish in advance. You also need to decide who will be responsible for feeding and cleaning up after your puppy. Who will take the puppy for walks? Who will take the puppy to his potty area after he eats? Who will pick up his toys, and who will be responsible for cleaning up the yard? The whole family can certainly participate in pet care duties, but the details should be worked out ahead of time to avoid protests and conflicts later.

OBTAINING SUPPLIES

Purchasing items for your future furry family member is one of the most fun and productive

DANGEROUS PLANTS

Plants that are toxic to your poodle puppy can be found both indoors and outdoors. Some of the common plants to keep out of your puppy's reach include:

Plant	Toxic Parts	Plant	Toxic Parts
Azaleas	Entire plant	Mistletoe	Berries
Daffodil	Bulbs	Philodendrons	Entire plant
Elephant's ear	Entire plant	Poinsettia	Leaves, stem, flowers
English ivy	Entire plant		
Foxglove	Leaves	Rhubarb	Leaves
Holly	Berries		
Hyacinth	Bulbs		
Iris	Leaves, roots		
Lily of the valley	Leaves, flowers		

For a full list of common poisonous plants, visit the Web site of the Humane Society of the United States, www.hsus.org.

ways to anticipate your puppy's arrival! Some of the items you can consider buying in advance include a collar, a leash, a crate, a dog bed, puppy food, chew toys, and food and water bowls. The abundant choices in designs are sure to offer something that sparks your interest, but don't sacrifice ease of maintenance for looks. Washable dog beds and dish-washer-safe food and water bowls will save you a lot of work and time in the long run.

BRINGING YOUR PUPPY HOME

When all the preparations have been made and the wonderful day has come to bring your new poodle puppy home, it's a time for celebration. But don't forget that your puppy is just a baby, and too much stimulation can cause stress, digestive upset, and a weakened immune system. So give your new puppy plenty of quiet time to recharge his batteries. You may have to limit his playtime with children or other dogs. The best time to bring your new puppy home is just before a weekend or a vacation, so you will have plenty of time to work with your puppy on household rules, establish a feeding and potty-break routine, and develop a bond with your new canine friend.

PUPPY NUTRITION

Up until the time your little fluff ball is eight weeks old, he should have access to his mother's milk. There is no dietary equivalent to the real thing, so let your puppy benefit from nature's diet until he is mature enough to be weaned.

Puppies can be introduced to soft foods when they are about four weeks old, and at six weeks old, they are ready to try dry commercial puppy foods. By the time they are eight weeks old, the amount of mother's milk they consume should have diminished considerably, and solid foods will have become the main source of their sustenance. Hopefully, your puppy's breeder has done her job up to this point by properly introducing your puppy to solid foods, so that he is well pre-

Many prepackaged dry foods have been scientifically formulated to provide your growing puppy with all the important nutrients he needs. By doing a little research, you can decide which brand or type of food will be best for your dog.

pared to leave his mother by the time you plan to take him home.

Growing puppies do have specific dietary needs, and these can only be

WATCH THAT DIET!

Your poodle puppy will have a lot of abrupt adjustments to make when you first bring him home, but a drastic change in his diet doesn't have to be one of them. Any sudden change in diet can cause digestive upset and diarrhea. This is even more pronounced in puppies that are under the additional stress of adjusting to a new environment—not a pleasant experience for you or your puppy! It's best to feed your puppy the same type of food he was receiving at the breeder's, at least for a few days after he comes home. After that, you can begin to gradually change his diet to the food of your choice.

met by feeding them a quality dog food especially formulated for puppies. You might also consider other diet options such as a bones and raw food (B.A.R.F.) diet, or a home-cooked diet. Just be sure to research these options thoroughly so that your growing puppy receives all the vitamins and minerals he needs.

Just as important as choosing a good-quality food is setting up a regular feeding schedule. If you're meticulous about feeding your poodle pup at the same times every day, this will have a tremendous effect on your puppy's elimination patterns, and that in turn will affect the success of your housetraining efforts! The frequency of feedings depends on your puppy's age, with puppies 8 to 12 weeks old requiring at least three feedings a day, and puppies over 12 weeks requiring two feedings a day. From then on, your dog will be happiest if he is fed twice a day throughout his adulthood.

Although it's important to socialize your puppy soon after you bring him home, always make sure your puppy is safe. Be sure to supervise your poodle pup when he is playing with young children.

COGNITIVE AND SOCIAL DEVELOPMENT

The first year of your puppy's life is not only a time for rapid physical growth, it is also a time for cognitive and social development. Your puppy's brain is constantly forming new associations as he learns new things, and it is believed by many in the dog-training profession that there are windows of opportunity when certain associations must be formed; if not, the opportunity for their development is virtually lost.

One of these vital associations is socialization to people. Studies at Jackson Laboratory in Bar Harbor, Maine, in 1961 indicated that puppies become irreversibly fearful of humans if they are denied sufficient human contact prior to the age of 12 weeks.

As noted by Stephen Budiansky in his book *The Truth About Dogs*, the results of this experiment do not necessarily prove that there is a "critical period" during which puppies have to be socialized to humans, as much as it demonstrates that the development of fear begins to "intervene and overpower" a puppy's capacity to socialize with humans.

These studies made it perfectly clear how important it is to socialize young puppies to humans in order for them to develop close attachments to people. This socialization, which consists of frequent interactions with and gentle handling by humans, should begin well before your puppy is ready to join your household. This is one of the most compelling reasons to get your puppy from a reputable breeder who has taken the time to handle and socialize your puppy since the day he was born.

But socialization to humans isn't the whole story. The same fear that can make a puppy shy away from humans can also make a puppy aversive to many other things, like other dogs or animals, strange objects, new places, noises, or just about any novel stimulus he encounters. In addition, any bad experiences your puppy has with any of these things during this fear-development stage can result in deep-rooted, lifelong

Introduce your puppy to all of the people and animals in and around your home. The more you socialize your puppy, the better. Here, a curious poodle meets a Golden Retriever.

antipathies. Avoid problems by continuing to socialize your puppy after he comes home, and promote his cognitive development by introducing your poodle puppy to as many different people, animals, places, and new situations as possible.

This is particularly important to remember for Toy and Miniature Poodles, some of which are perfectly content to limit their territory to their own homes. They need to go for walks to meet the neighbors, visit the park to play fetch, and stroll around other places that will allow them to experience more of the outside world. If you do this for your puppy, you will help him grow into a self-assured, confident animal, and there will be much less chance that he will develop problems with fearfulness or aggression.

GROOMING YOUR POODLE

Grooming is another experience that should be presented to your puppy at a young age, so he can become accustomed to it. This is particularly important for poodles, because their coats require quite a bit of maintenance. A poodle that does not tolerate grooming well makes life miserable both for himself and for his owner.

As soon as you bring your puppy home, get in the habit of handling his body parts. Hold his paw in your

FAST FACT

Poodles are the most creatively groomed canines on earth. Their hair has been used as a medium for sculpture, and they have been dyed and painted every color in the rainbow. The possibilities are endless!

hand for a second or two before you release it. Run your hands over his back, sides, and stomach. Hold his face in your hands. Play with his tail and ears occasionally. This will help desensitize your puppy to being touched on different parts of his body, because poodle grooming requires contact with just about every square inch of the dog. Hopefully, such preparation will make your puppy's first clipping

Get your puppy used to being handled and groomed by handling him yourself. This way, he associates grooming with love, rather than fear.

experience less stressful and eventually help him accept the grooming process with the patience and confidence of a veteran show dog.

Your puppy should have his first clipping by 12 weeks of age. If you wait any longer than that, his curly locks may grow into a tangled and unmanageable mess! Your puppy needs to learn to tolerate the noise and vibration of electric clippers, the routine of bathing, and the "wind" of a hair dryer, and he will accept these things much more easily if he is exposed to them by this age. After that, a trim every six to eight weeks will keep him looking and feeling great.

Most poodle owners choose the services of a professional groomer to take care of their poodle's clipping needs, but you can learn to do it yourself if you are so inclined. The most authoritative resource on poodle clipping is Shirlee Kalstone's book *Poodle Clipping and Grooming: The International Reference.* Keep in mind that grooming your own poodle will

DO-IT-YOURSELF GROOMING

Clipping your own poodle may seem like a monumental and intimidating task, but simple pet clips are surprisingly easy to do. The right tools can make this job even easier, but they do represent a considerable initial investment. The following are the minimum equipment requirements to get started:

Electric clipper
Clipper blades or adapters
Slicker brush
Comb
Nail clipper
Hemostat (for plucking the ears)
Straight shears (scissors)
Grooming table
Hair dryer
Dog shampoo

Dog conditioner
Tub or sink mat
Bath towels
Spray nozzle
Grooming
 instruction book

A slicker brush is a necessary tool for any dog owner.

require a considerable investment in tools, and it will also take some practice to become expert at it.

If you'd rather not deal with the mess and fuss of clipping your own poodle, you can find a professional groomer by asking your friends, your breeder, or your veterinarian for references. You can also locate groomers in the phone book and then visit them in person to get pricing information. This will give you a chance to evaluate the conditions at the grooming shop, note the groomer's professional attitude, and possibly observe the groomer at work to see how she treats the dogs in her charge.

INTERIM GROOMING

It is easy and convenient to pay a professional groomer to take care of clipping your poodle, but don't get the wrong idea—this does not absolve you of all grooming responsibilities. Your poodle will still require some interim maintenance to keep him in good condition between visits to the groomer. This will require, at minimum, the purchase of a slicker brush (a flat brush with rows of thin wire teeth), a comb, and nail clippers. Your poodle may also get into a sticky, messy, or smelly situation at some time, necessitating a bath in between his regular grooming

appointments. Be prepared for this by having the right equipment on hand—a spray nozzle (one that fits a sink faucet for a Toy or Miniature Poodle, or one that fits a bathtub shower fixture for a Standard Poodle), a rubber mat for the tub or sink, and dog shampoo.

Brushing your poodle once a week will help prevent the formation of mats, and the neater you keep your poodle's hair, the better job your professional groomer will be able to do. You can maintain your poodle's fleecelike appearance by "back brushing" (brushing against the natural lay of the coat) and lifting the brush straight up at the end of your strokes. This will separate the ringlets into individual hairs and turn your poodle's curly coat into a solid fluff. Your comb will come in handy to comb out any minor mats, especially the mats that plague his ears.

NAIL CARE

Some poodles' nails require clipping every three to four weeks, so you may also have to do some nail clipping in between professional grooming sessions. Inexpensive nail clippers can be purchased at any pet supply store, and some come with a metal nail file that can be used to file off any rough nail edges.

The clipper should be held perpendicular to the nail, and then the tip of the nail can be clipped off. You must be careful not to cut into the quick, which supplies blood to the nail; this can cause pain and profuse bleeding. The quick is visible as a dark core inside light-colored nails. On a dark-colored poodle with black nails, you will have to estimate the location of the quick by looking at the hook of the nail and judging how much nail is excess.

Nail clipping can be an intimidating procedure, so if you don't feel comfortable doing it, not to worry.

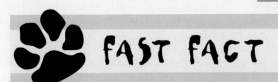

FAST FACT

Overgrown nails can adversely affect a poodle's entire body. Long nails that cause pain to the foot can make a dog lame, which in turn causes stress and strain on the leg, which affects the dog's posture, which then can cause back or hip problems. So keep your poodle's nails trimmed!

Veterinarians and professional groomers are usually willing to take care of this responsibility for a very modest fee.

BATHING

Although the process of washing a dog is no more complicated than washing your own hair, a few tricks can help you perform this job more efficiently and comfortably. First, try to untangle any matted hair before bathing, as mats become tighter and more difficult to brush out after the hair gets wet. A good brushing before bathing will save you time in the long run.

Second, make sure you have all your supplies ready—shampoo,

Speak calmly and reward your poodle with praise or a treat when he lets you clip his nails. By showing your dog there is no reason to get upset, he will learn in time that nail clipping is nothing to fear.

spray nozzle, cream rinse (if desired), tub or sink mat, cotton balls (to keep water out of your dog's ears), and towels—before getting your dog wet. You don't want to find yourself with a wet dog in the sink when the shampoo or towels are out of reach!

And third, when initially wetting your dog, wet his feet and legs first so he can adjust to the water temperature gradually. You are also best off waiting to wash your poodle's head until you've finished washing his body. The instant your dog's head gets wet, he'll have an urge to shake, so save this body part for last! Then, when you're done washing his head, you can cover him up quickly with a towel so you can avoid getting drenched.

There are dozens of dog shampoos on the market. Some are

Bathing your poodle at home can be a big undertaking. If you aren't sure you can handle the job, there are many dog grooming companies that offer bathing and grooming services at a reasonable cost. Some even have mobile units that will come to your home, saving you the trouble of transporting your dog to the facility.

designed to enhance colors. Others have added scents, or treat various skin and coat types or conditions. But unless their use is advised by your veterinarian or you're looking toward showing your dog, choose the mildest form of shampoo. It's the least likely to cause reactions.

After his bath, you can let your puppy air dry and fluff him up later with your slicker brush, or you can use a hair dryer to expedite the drying process. If you opt for the hair dryer, use a low-heat, low-air setting, because human hair dryers can get very hot and uncomfortable, and they can be very loud and startling to a young pup. You will also need to find a suitable and safe place to dry your dog. Any table or countertop with a nonslip mat will work for a Toy or Miniature Poodle, provided your dog can be kept from jumping off and injuring himself. Otherwise, it might be better to do this job on the floor, where it's easiest to dry the Standard Poodle. Back brushing while drying your poodle with a hair dryer will add volumes of fluff to your dog's hairdo.

EAR CARE

Like many other floppy-eared dogs, the poodle is prone to ear infections, thanks to a lack of air circulation around the ear canals. The long, thick hair of the ears and the hair that grows inside the poodle's ear canals make this problem worse by trapping moisture inside the ear. It helps to keep your dog's ears as dry as possible during baths by placing cotton balls inside them, but regular ear cleanings should also be performed.

You should swab your dog's ears regularly with cotton balls that have been lightly moistened with rubbing alcohol. The alcohol helps to dry out the ear canals. The hair inside the ear canals should be plucked out during regular grooming sessions every six to eight weeks.

You can detect ear problems early by checking your poodle's ears frequently. Signs of an ear infection include cracked, red, sore, or itchy skin on the underside of the earflap. But the most noticeable symptoms will be the scratching and discomfort exhibited by your dog, and the unmistakable odor emanating from his ears. If your poodle appears to have an ear infection, a trip to the veterinarian for treatment is definitely in order.

DENTAL CARE

Canine personal hygiene doesn't begin and end with hair care. Dental care is just as important. According to the American Veterinary Dental Association, 80 percent of dogs over the age of three suffer from some degree of gum disease. This isn't surprising when you consider the diet of domestic dogs. Canned dog foods tend to stick to the teeth and cause tartar and plaque buildup, and commercial dry foods crack and crumble before they can scrape the teeth clean near the gum line. Compare this to the diet of wild dogs, which includes bones, tendons, and entrails that serve as nature's dental floss and teeth scrapers.

Certainly, some chew products are helpful in keeping dogs' teeth clean, but, unfortunately, poodles are not known to be very strong chew-

ers, so they may not get the greatest benefit from these products. Toy and Miniature Poodles, like other small dogs, are particularly prone to dental problems. Receding gums is a symptom of periodontal disease that is common among smaller poodles. Your vet may prescribe an antibiotic to help treat this problem.

The best way to prevent your poodle from developing periodontal disease is to brush his teeth. Canine toothbrushes and toothpastes are now available at most pet supply outlets, and most dogs can be taught to tolerate having their teeth brushed

Brushing your dog's teeth may seem like an unusual task. However, when this is done regularly it prevents dental problems and can help eliminate dog breath.

fairly easily. Because canine toothpastes are designed to taste good to dogs, all you need to add is a little bit of patience and gentle handling. (For Toy or Miniature Poodles, with their tiny teeth and small mouths, you may find it easier to place a little toothpaste on your finger and gently rub it over his teeth and gums.)

Try to brush your poodle's teeth at least once a week, and preferably more often. If you incorporate dental care into your grooming routine, you'll realize how little time this responsibility demands. Its benefits, however, are enormous. Regular dental care at home helps prevent the loss of teeth and oral infections that can lead to serious health problems, and may reduce or eliminate the need for more invasive dental care by your veterinarian. (However, even with regular brushing, you may need to have your poodle's teeth cleaned annually by your veterinarian.) And brushing your pet's teeth at home can even help prevent one of the most offensive odors on earth—dog breath. Is there any better reason to take your dog's dental health seriously?

TRAINING

Providing health care, nutrition, socialization, and grooming for your puppy is sure to keep your puppy happy. But what about you? If you

want to be just as content as your puffy pooch, you need to invest some time and effort in training him. Your puppy has already learned from his mother and littermates about getting along with other dogs, but he needs to learn how to be a good companion for humans, too.

ESTABLISHING RULES OF BEHAVIOR

Your puppy may engage in certain habits that are quite acceptable to other dogs, but are not as acceptable to you. Puppies jump on each other in greeting and play. They nip at each other and steal things from each other. Poodle puppies can be exceptionally energetic and they participate in these kinds of behaviors with gusto. If you don't appreciate these behaviors, you need to enforce rules against them from the very beginning. Everyone in the household, likewise, should be involved in enforcing these rules so that your puppy will be treated consistently.

Behaviors that may seem adorable when your puppy is little can eventually become serious annoyances as your puppy grows. So think ahead. If you don't think you'll appreciate having your adult dog greet you by jumping on your legs, don't let your puppy jump on you,

Poodles respond to both visual and aural commands, but don't forget about the power of treats! When training your dog, it's okay to reward him for a job well done. He will eventually associate responding to your commands with a positive reward. Soon you won't have to have a treat in hand. The keys are patience and practice.

even in play. If you don't want your dog to bite people when he gets older, don't let your puppy nip at your hands, feet, or face.

You should let your puppy know what you don't like by issuing a firm "No!" or "Uh-uh!" and then redirecting him to another activity, like playing with one of his toys. If your pup refuses to desist, you can abruptly refuse to play with him. The most effective punishment for a puppy is to take away his fun and attention by ignoring him!

HOUSETRAINING

Housetraining is the most important training your puppy will need to become a good household pet and roommate. The process of housetraining can be much less frustrating if you have realistic expectations and utilize your dog's natural instincts to accomplish the task.

Toy Poodles, like other toy dogs, may take up to a year to fully housetrain. This characteristic of very small dogs has been explained as a possible difference in maturity rate, or a difference in perspective due to the dog's short stature. Whatever the reason, Toy Poodle owners should be prepared to take considerably longer to housetrain their dogs. Standard Poodles, on the other hand, may need only a few weeks to a couple of months, and Miniature Poodles generally fall somewhere in between.

Until your puppy is reliably housetrained, you should expect occasional accidents, but these can be minimized with proper supervision and management. Your puppy has a natural instinct to eliminate wherever there are odors of prior eliminations. This means you must thoroughly clean the floor where accidents have occurred, using a

In time your poodle will catch on to the concept of eliminating outside always, no matter what the weather is like.

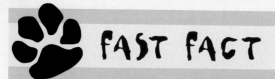

product that will help neutralize the scent, such as an enzymatic cleaner. (These are available at pet supply stores.) You can use this instinct to your advantage, too, by choosing an outdoor potty area where the scents of previous use will encourage your puppy to continue using it.

Dogs usually sniff the ground and turn around several times, searching for a suitable spot to eliminate, so if your puppy displays this behavior you know it's time to rush him outside. Dogs also tend to eliminate shortly after eating or sleeping, so these are ideal times to take your puppy to his outside potty area.

If your puppy does have an accident, don't punish him! A housetraining lapse just means your puppy hasn't yet learned where he is supposed to go, or he hasn't learned how to communicate to you that he needs to go outside. It's not fair or fruitful to punish your puppy for something he doesn't know. Instead, rush him outside as quickly as possible and then clean up the mess without a fuss. With time, patience, and practice, your puppy will catch on.

CRATE TRAINING

The virtues of crates have made crate training a very popular form of education for young dogs. A crate is good for confining a dog for short periods. It can help keep a dog safe during car travel. It can make a nice "escape" for a dog that needs a refuge from overstimulating activity. And it is so much more pleasant to use a crate when a dog is trained to tolerate this type of confinement, rather than fussing, barking, and whining to get out.

Crate training relies on your dog's natural instinct to lie down in a small space, a primitive behavior left over from the dog's wild, den-dwelling days. This training is a gradual process that involves encouraging your puppy to go into his crate willingly by placing toys or treats inside. When your puppy shows no fear of his crate, he can be fed in his crate or given a chew toy to enjoy while inside it. Eventually, your puppy can be confined to his crate for successively longer periods.

Introduce your puppy to his crate in a positive way. As he grows he may come to know it as his "home," so it's important to keep any references to the crate positive. Make sure the crate is a proper size for your dog; while this crate would be appropriate for a Standard Poodle, it's murch too large for a Toy or Miniature Poodle.

There are two keys to successful crate training: don't rush it, and don't abuse the crate. You must not push the training process faster than the comfort level of your puppy, or you will make him fearful or distrustful. And you must not use the crate to punish your puppy or to confine him for extended periods, or he will learn to associate the crate with negative experiences. If you need to leave your puppy alone for more than a couple of hours, you should confine him to a larger area, preferably with access to his crate for sleeping.

🐾 🐾 🐾

Preparing for your puppy will add to the thrill of bringing him home. You will be able to welcome your poodle with confidence and eagerness. And your puppy, too, will be much more comfortable during his transition, as he becomes the new member of your family.

CHAPTER SIX

Things to Know as Your Puppy Grows (Six Months to Two Years)

The poodle puppy that used to follow you everywhere like a tagalong sibling sometimes doesn't seem to care as much about where you are and what you're doing. The same puppy that ran enthusiastically to you every time you called his name now ignores you from time to time. What happened? Did your poodle's personality change? No, he's simply growing up!

Puppies between the ages of six months and two years go through a developmental stage that is often

As your poodle grows, you will begin to see his personality develop and mature.

likened to the "terrible twos" or the "teenage years" in humans. Up to this point, your puppy sought the constant comfort and assurance of his surrogate mother—you—but now he needs to do more exploring on his own so he can learn about the world around him. Unfortunately, he also needs to test the limits you have set for him in order to learn how much control he has over his environment and the people and animals in it.

During this period your poodle will reach his adult height and his physical growth rate will slow considerably, but don't let this fool you. Your poodle is still growing both physically and mentally. Additional bone and muscle growth will continue up to the age of two, and the "terrible twos" may last just as long.

GROWTH PATTERNS

Toy and Miniature Poodles reach their mature height at six to eight months old, while Standard Poodles may take up to 12 months to fully mature. (The fact that small dogs don't have quite as much growing to do as larger dogs may account for this difference.) Recent genetic studies have identified the gene responsible for controlling the adult size of dogs, and this gene could very well determine at what point growth stops.

Although your poodle may look mature, it's important to keep enforcing the training you've already started to continue his mental development.

Because of the muscle, bone, and joint development that continues until the age of two, you should not overwork your poodle (or allow him to overwork himself, as poodles sometimes like to do) during this time. Activities that put excessive strain on your dog's developing structure, such as constant leaping or hard running, can damage his joints, causing problems that are not easy or inexpensive to repair.

VACCINATIONS

By now, your puppy has received a complete series of puppy vaccinations, but his system has not yet built up complete immunity to these diseases. He'll need one more booster at one year of age before he can advance to the recommended three-year boosters for adult dogs.

NUTRITION

Because smaller poodles mature sooner physically than their standard-sized counterparts, Toy and Miniature Poodles can usually be switched to an adult formula dog food by the age of ten months. Standard Poodles should remain on puppy food until they are a full year old. In either case, if you keep your dog on a high-calorie puppy food longer than necessary, it may result in unwanted weight gain, so keep an eye on your dog's weight as he approaches a year of age.

When your puppy is ready for adult dog food, choose a quality brand of food. The importance of this choice cannot be overstated. Even though high-quality foods are more

VACCINATION SCHEDULE (6 MONTHS-ADULT)

The following vaccination schedule is recommended by the American Animal Hospital Association:

Vaccine	Age for Boosters
Distemper	1 year, then every 3 years
Parvovirus	1 year, then every 3 years
Parainfluenza	1 year, then every 3 years
Coronavirus	1 year, then every 3 years
Canine adenovirus-2	1 year, then every 3 years
Leptospirosis	1 year, then every 3 years
Bordetella *	1 year, then as needed
Lyme disease *	1 year, then prior to tick season
Rabies +	1 year, then every 3 years

* Optional vaccines, depending on location and risk.
+ Required by law. Some states still require annual boosters.

Source: American Animal Hospital Association

expensive by weight, they are made with better ingredients, which are more easily absorbed and utilized by the dog's body. This means it takes a smaller amount of high-quality food to provide the same amount of energy and nutrients as a poorer-quality food. A true cost comparison will reveal that it doesn't cost much more to feed your dog a high-quality brand than an economy brand of food. But the clear difference in your dog's lustrous coat, shining eyes, and healthy energy level will be undeniable.

FEEDING PRACTICES

Feeding your poodle a high-quality food is just one of the feeding practices that influences your dog's weight and nutritional health. Measuring your dog's food, feeding him at regular times each day, and keeping him from eating too many treats and too much "people food" can also help prevent weight gain and nutritional deficiencies.

Because your dog is still growing at this stage, his calorie needs will fluctuate with his growth spurts. You need to measure your dog's food (any type of scoop or cup will work for this purpose), monitor your dog's

weight, observe your dog's eating habits, and adjust the amount you feed him accordingly. If your dog leaves some food in his dish when he's done eating, or if he takes longer than 20 minutes to eat his meal, you can reduce the amount you feed him. If he finishes his meal very quickly and seems to be looking for more food, this may be a sign that you need to feed him more.

It might seem convenient to leave a bowl of food out all day so your dog can eat whenever he wants, but "free feeding," as this practice is called, encourages poor eating habits. If your dog is allowed

What you feed your poodle is as important as *when, how much,* and *how often.*

to snack during the day, he will consume more calories than he needs. Such irregular eating habits can also contribute to housetraining lapses. So give your dog 20 minutes to eat his meal, and then remove his dish until the next scheduled feeding time.

Your dog's weight is not only determined by how much he eats, but also by *what* he eats. Adding people food to your dog's diet and feeding him treats are practices that should be done in moderation. Your dog will no doubt appreciate a special treat now and then, but pay attention to how much of his balanced diet is being replaced by unhealthy types of food.

Poodles are notoriously finicky eaters, so it's not a good idea to get in the habit of adding people food or other enhancements to your poodle's meals. Poodles are very intelligent and can become quite manipulative. It won't take your poodle long to figure out that if he refuses to eat his dog food, you'll give him something yummy. Avoid this problem by adhering to a relatively strict diet.

If you want to give your poodle something to make his meal more palatable, give him a little canned food along with his dry rations. Your

FIT AND TRIM

It is estimated that 25 to 44 percent of dogs in the United States are obese. Healthy feeding practices can help keep your dog trim:

- Feed your dog a high-quality dog food.
- Measure your dog's food.
- Monitor your dog's weight and adjust the amount you feed him accordingly.
- Feed your dog twice a day on a regular schedule.
- Remove any uneaten food after 20 minutes.
- Avoid enhancing your dog's meal with people food.
- Limit treats and edible chew products.

CHECKING YOUR DOG'S WEIGHT

Your poodle's fluffy hair can easily make him appear chubby even when he's not, so it can be difficult to tell if your dog is getting too portly or too skinny for his own good. The easiest way to tell if your dog is tipping the scales in the wrong direction is to feel his ribs. If you can feel your dog's ribs through a moderate layer of protective fat, your dog is a good weight. If you have to press into your dog's sides in order to feel his ribs, he needs to cut back on his kibble. If your dog's ribs are noticeably protruding, he is underweight. This may indicate that you need to feed him more, or it may be a sign of a medical problem. It's good to get into the habit of checking your dog's weight regularly during your grooming sessions.

poodle will appreciate the different texture and flavor, and you won't have to worry about spoiling his diet. In particular, Toy and Miniature Poodles prefer softer foods and smaller kibble than do larger breeds.

If your young poodle does gain a little too much weight, don't use a low-calorie diet dog food to address the problem. These foods are not only low in fat, they are also low in protein, which can cause your growing dog to lose muscle mass. At this age, the best way to handle excess weight is to cut back on your dog's regular rations and add more exercise to his daily routine.

SOCIALIZATION

Throughout your puppy's first two years, he is growing socially as well as physically. Even though your puppy has outgrown the fear development stage, you still need to expose him to as many people, objects, sights, and sounds as possible. This education is vitally important throughout your dog's life. But the new development of a "teenage" canine attitude can be challenging and frustrating to handle.

Your poodle is becoming more independent, and because of this he doesn't seem to listen very well. He'll test you to see what he can get away with, and he'll get into more mischief as his boldness and curiosity grow. He'll even test any other pets in the household to see how much of his silly behavior they will tolerate. All of this is bound to cause some conflicts and upheaval in the household.

While it's still a good idea to socialize your puppy as much as possible during his adolescent stage, he must be corrected when he tries to test his limits by displaying inappropriate behavior.

This is a time when you must be a patient pet parent. You need to enforce your authority firmly but gently during this critical development period, and you can take solace in the fact that your pup will eventually outgrow that obstinate attitude as he matures.

BASIC OBEDIENCE TRAINING

Obedience training is one of the best ways to teach your dog to trust and respect you. You have already established and enforced household rules, which is a good start. You may have also started to work with your puppy on basic obedience commands. Now is the time to practice obedience training on a regular basis if you don't already do so.

Your poodle is amazingly bright, and you would be missing out on a great deal of fun if you didn't devote some time each week to training

FAST FACT

Basic obedience skills can easily be taught at home, but formal obedience classes can help sharpen those skills, making your dog more responsive to your commands. In addition, the guidance of a professional trainer is invaluable, especially if you need to address certain problem behaviors.

him! Training is also a great bonding activity, because you and your dog will learn to communicate with each other and work together as a team. Your dog's intelligence, combined with his strong, innate desire to please you, means he is exceptionally easy to train—even during this challenging developmental period.

SIT: The most natural, and therefore the easiest, command to teach your dog is "sit." Dogs are very comfortable sitting, so it doesn't take much to coax your dog into this position using a "lure and reward" method. You can "lure" your dog into this position by holding a treat just above his head and moving the treat behind your dog's eye level. As your dog leans backward to keep his eyes on the treat, he will most likely drop automatically into a sit. If he does, reward him immediately with the treat. By

adding the command "sit" as your dog does this, your dog will quickly learn what is expected of him.

DOWN: Once your dog has mastered "sit," the next logical position to teach him is "down." With your dog already sitting, you can lure him into a down position by holding a treat on the floor in front of him. As your dog bends down to sniff the treat, move the treat a little farther away to encourage him to stretch out his front legs toward the treat. If he stretches out even a little bit, even

Training a dog to sit takes time and patience.

though he's not in a full down position, reward him. With each successive attempt, you can ask your dog to stretch out a little farther until he eventually achieves the full down position. Once your dog reaches this point, add the command "down," so that he can learn to associate the command with this position.

STAY: The "stay" is an exercise that involves increasing both duration and distance. Successfully teaching the stay depends on starting out with very short durations and distances and gradually working up to longer ones. Instruct your dog to sit, and then ask him to stay. If he doesn't move for just a second, reward him! The next time you ask your dog to stay, wait until he holds the stay for two seconds before you reward him. The time after

"Down" and "stay" are helpful commands that can help keep your poodle out of trouble.

that, wait three seconds, and so on, to help increase his duration.

You can work on distance by telling your dog to stay and taking one quick step away from him. If he maintains his stay, step toward your dog and reward him. When he is proficient in maintaining the stay when you take one step away, try taking two steps away. Reward your dog each time he doesn't move. In this way, you can increase the distance gradually until you can eventually leave the room while your dog stays seated.

The important thing to keep in mind when working on distance is that you must walk back to your dog to reward him. If you tell your dog to come to you so you can reward him, your dog will learn very quickly that "stay" means "stay for a little while and then come." Be sure to practice the "stay" and "come" commands separately to avoid this problem. If your dog breaks his stay when you are practicing either duration or distance, you need to regress a step in your training until your dog is more consistent at a shorter duration or distance.

COME: "Come" is the most important, but also the most challenging, command to teach your dog. A dog that doesn't come reliably when he's called is an accident waiting to happen. That's why this command should be practiced constantly, at all times and in all places. Your young poodle may be a little stubborn in responding to this command, but fortunately, poodles have very strong attachments to their owners. They like to be where their people are, and they absolutely love to make their owners happy. Use these traits to your advantage to instill a strong response to "come."

Keep some treats in your pocket and call your dog at various intervals during the day. Reward your dog each time he comes. Call your dog only once each time so that he can learn to come on the first call—he gets no rewards if he doesn't come the first time! When your dog is consistent in responding to the "come" command in your home, it's time to practice the come command outside, where there are more distractions.

You must be able to enforce your commands if your dog doesn't listen, so if your dog doesn't come when you call, you must go get him. If you can't enforce this command when your dog is off his leash, you may need to practice it while your dog is on a long leash. Then, if he doesn't come, go get your dog and bring him to the place from where you called him. Do not pull him to you by the leash, as your brilliant poodle will decide that compliance to the come

FAST FACT

If your young dog gets loose and won't come when you call him (those "teenage" dogs can be stinkers), try coaxing him into chasing you by running away from him. Or ask him a question that might get his interest, like, "Do you want a treat?" "Wanna go for a ride?" or, "Wanna play ball?" and then reward him with whatever you promised if he comes to you.

command is only compulsory when he is on a leash!

If you practice this command constantly and enforce it consistently, you can condition your dog to respond automatically, which should be your ultimate goal. Your "teenage" dog may frustrate you at times, but there is no substitute for maturity. Most dogs become much more responsive to the come command as they outgrow this wild phase of puppyhood. In the long run, all the work (and fun!) of training your dog will be worth it, as the pot of gold at the end of the rainbow is a well-mannered poodle that you can enjoy and take pride in for many years to come.

TRAVELING WITH YOUR POODLE

One of the few problems with getting tangled up in a poodle's ties of devotion is that you might find it difficult to leave your poodle behind when you need to travel. Poodles are for people who like to include their dogs in everything they do, so go ahead and plan to take your puffy pooch with you! This is amazingly easy to do with Toy and Miniature Poodles, as their size makes them extremely portable. But even the substantial Standard Poodle is a wonderful traveling companion. This is illustrated in John Steinbeck's book *Travels with Charley: In Search of America*, which chronicles the author's travels with his Standard Poodle, Charley.

TRAVELING BY CAR

Most poodles love hitting the road, and your poodle may very well express his delight and excitement at the prospect of going for a ride. But if your dog is not accustomed to traveling in a crate, seat carrier, or doggy seat belt, you should take the time to acquaint your dog with these safety devices. If you use one every time you put your dog in a vehicle, he will learn to associate it with the excitement of travel and adventure.

Be sure to make any lodging arrangements in advance, as not all hotels and motels are pet-friendly. There are several resources and Web sites that can help you locate appropriate lodging for you and your dog, including www.petswelcome.com and www.travelpets.com. Some establishments do make exceptions to their

Poodles love to do everything their humans do—including riding in the car!

TRAVEL SAFETY

Traveling with your dog is fun, as long as you keep your dog safe!

- Make sure your dog is up-to-date on vaccinations.

- Obtain any additional vaccinations your dog may need, depending on your travel destination. Will you be staying where Lyme disease is prevalent?

- Bring a photo of your dog, together with any health documentation, such as a rabies vaccination certificate.

- Keep a collar and ID tag on your dog at all times, and keep your dog on a leash.

- Make sure your dog is microchipped prior to your trip.

- Don't forget to bring any medications your dog requires.

- A canine first aid kit is a must for campers.

"no pets" policies, especially for well behaved, nonshedding breeds like the poodle, so it never hurts to ask.

When you've embarked on a trip, it's always frustrating to discover that you've forgotten something. So make a list of the pet care items you'll need to bring for your poodle, and double-check the list before you leave. You'll need an ample supply of dog food, collar and ID tags, leashes, food and water bowls, and waste collection bags. It is also wise to bring a brush and comb, because poodle hair is notorious for collecting debris. You'll need treats and toys to keep your dog happy and occupied while traveling. For safety's sake, bring a photo of your dog, along with his

health and identification information, in case he gets lost or suffers a medical emergency.

While on the road, you can keep your dog happy and comfortable by giving him plenty of opportunities to take potty breaks, stretch his legs, and get drinks of water. Never leave your dog unattended in a closed vehicle, especially in warmer climates. On a 73° Fahrenheit (23° Celsius) day, the temperature inside a car can reach 120°F (49°C) in 30 minutes. On a 90°F (32°C) day, the temperature can reach 160°F (71°C) in less than 15 minutes. If you must leave your dog alone in your vehicle for a short period, keep the air conditioner running or use a window fan

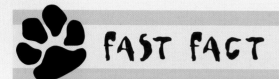

(available in pet catalogs and some pet supply stores) to help provide good air circulation.

TRAVELING BY AIR

Most of these same preparations are required if you travel by air, but plane travel has its own considerations. Additional preparations include contacting the airline at least a few weeks in advance to find out what the travel requirements are for your dog, and checking out any quarantine procedures or required vaccinations if you're traveling out of the country. Airlines have specifications for the size and type of pet carriers that are allowed. They will also provide rules and instructions for the safe air travel of your pet.

Because of current airport security procedures, your pet carrier may need to be inspected. Any time your dog needs to be removed from his carrier, there is a risk of his escape, which would be a truly frightening experience for both you and your dog. For this reason, you should insist that inspections be carried out only in your presence so you can keep control of your dog. Afterwards, use plastic fasteners to make sure your dog's carrier is securely closed.

ALTERNATIVE CARE FOR YOUR POODLE

In a perfect world, you could take your poodle with you wherever you went and you would enjoy all of life's experiences together. But there are occasions when it's just not appropriate to bring your dog along. You might get more than a few odd stares if you arrived at a wedding, a funeral, or a business meeting with your pup in tow. In cases like this, it's important to have a backup plan. Who will take care of your dog when you can't?

BOARDING KENNELS: There are still a few "traditional" boarding kennels, with cold, foreboding kennel runs as sparse in amenities as prison cells. But in recent years many boarding kennels have become much more appealing to humans and much more comfortable for dogs. These establishments offer customized care according to each dog's individual needs, and even provide social activities for the dogs, like group playtimes. When you need extended care for your dog, it doesn't hurt to investigate local boarding kennels to find out the range of their services.

A physical inspection of the boarding facility is a must. Does the staff seem knowledgeable? Do they handle the dogs with respect? Are the kennels clean and dry? Do all the dogs have fresh water and soft bedding? First impressions are usually correct, so if a boarding kennel makes you feel uncomfortable, stressed, or anxious, you should take your business elsewhere or consider another pet care option, such as a pet sitter.

PET SITTERS: Pet sitters are available to care for your dog when you're out of town on business trips or vacations, but they can also help care for your dog at other times. Work schedules can make it difficult to meet your dog's needs. Long hours, odd shifts, or last-minute meetings can present challenges in keeping your dog on a reasonable schedule.

A pet sitter will care for your dog in your own home. She can provide midday dog walks or administer medications during the day. She can come to your home several times a day to care for your dog when you're on vacation, which allows your dog

The Web site of the National Association of Professional Pet Sitters, www.petsitters.org, can be used to help you find the right person to watch your pet while you're away.

to remain in a familiar, comfortable environment while you're gone. In addition, if you ask, your pet sitter may also be willing to provide housesitting services, like bringing in the mail, watering the plants, and deterring thieves by turning the lights on at night.

A good start in locating a reputable pet sitter is to check with the National Association of Professional Pet Sitters for referrals. You should meet in person with anyone you consider entrusting with your dog and the keys to your home. The pet sitter should show a lot of interest in your dog and ask a lot of questions about his habits, health, and needs.

DOGGY DAY CARE: American work habits have also spawned doggy day care centers, which are akin to day care centers for children. As the name implies, they provide daytime care for dogs while their owners are at work. Although few dog owners would consider putting their dogs in

day care on a daily basis, many find that using this service several times a week or month is very beneficial for active dogs. It helps dogs expend some of their energy in positive ways, and it also gives them opportunities for social interaction.

Poodles definitely have plenty of energy reserves to expend, but some poodles may be too nervous or high-strung to tolerate the boisterous activity at a doggy day care center. You need to consider your individual dog's temperament and size to determine if he's a good candidate

Since your poodle can't accompany you to the office, a doggy day care center may be a better option than leaving him home alone all day. These facilities can ensure that he gets the attention he needs—even when you're at work.

for the doggy day care experience, and then you'll need to evaluate the doggy day care center you're considering to be sure it's a good match for your dog. For example, Toy Poodles may be injured if they are put into day care with larger dogs, so you'll have to find a doggy day care center that offers programs for little dogs.

A quality doggy day care center will have staff experienced in handling dogs. The best day care will have ample supervision for the dogs (no more than 10 dogs per staff member), a rigorous screening procedure to make sure that all of the dogs can get along, and safeguards to prevent dogs from escaping from the facility. The services offered at some doggy day cares have expanded to include veterinary services, professional grooming, canine massage, and aromatherapy. It is probably just a matter of time before they're routinely called "doggy day spas!"

❧ ❧ ❧

Providing your puppy with the proper care, nutrition, socialization, and training will help you mold him into the perfect companion dog. This requires a considerable commitment in time and resources, but what you get out of it is priceless—a dog that loves and respects you to the ends of the earth.

CHAPTER SEVEN

Caring for Your Adult Poodle

The first two years of your puppy's life can be busy, challenging, and also very rewarding. You have watched your puppy grow from a carefree bundle of energy and curls into a refined and dignified member of your family. You have invested the care and training necessary to turn your poodle into a fine companion, and now you get to enjoy the fruits of your investment!

HEALTH ISSUES

Hereditary health issues are like time-release capsules. Some problems appear at a younger age while others are late-onset conditions. One symptom you should watch for during

Poodles require regular exercise, and will look forward to spending a day at the park with you.

your poodle's adulthood is limping or skipping with the hind legs, which may indicate hip dysplasia in Standard Poodles or a luxating patella in Toy or Miniature Poodles. Also look out for signs of eye irritations or vision loss, which could be due to a variety of eye conditions known to affect poodles.

Nonhereditary health issues are concerns during any life stage. If you're alert, you can pick up ear infections, parasite infestations, tooth problems, other illnesses, and injuries at an early stage, when they can be treated most effectively. Many minor conditions can become considerably worse with neglect, so don't ignore any condition that appears to be abnormal.

At this age, your dog has developed a much stronger immunity to the diseases for which he has been vaccinated, which means booster vaccinations can be reduced to three-year intervals. However, you should still take your dog to the vet for annual checkups. Preventatives for heartworm and bordetella still have to be prescribed or administered by your vet on an annual basis.

EXERCISE

One of the reasons dog owners tend to be healthier than those who don't own dogs is because it's impossible to walk a dog while sitting on a couch. You can reap your own health benefits by providing regular exercise for your dog. Taking your dog for a walk and playing fetch on a daily basis shouldn't be considered chores. Think of these activities as quality bonding time with your poodle, and enjoy these opportunities to enrich your relationship.

Walking is more than good exercise. It provides social opportunities

Make walking with your poodle a regular habit. It's good for both of you!

that constantly reinforce your dog's good manners, since you'll likely meet other dogs and people while you're out walking. It provides distractions you can use to practice obedience skills and teach your dog self-control. It's also a good way to satisfy your dog's need to explore and stimulate his senses.

Playing fetch or tug are activities that provide more than fun for your poodle. A good aerobic workout strengthens his cardiovascular system and relieves his stress by allowing him to expend his stockpile of energy. A poodle that doesn't have a daily outlet for his exuberance may very well erupt in wild and uncontrollable ways! But if your poodle can count on regular physical activity, he'll be a much happier and better-behaved dog.

The poodle loves to stretch his physical abilities to their limits, but as an intellectual breed he also thrives on mental challenges. There are many dog sports and activities that combine both training and exercise to give your dog well-rounded experiences. Just as children who participate in sports or volunteer activities develop character, so it is with dogs. If you want to take your dog's training to the next level, investigate the many wonderful options.

ADVANCED TRAINING AND ACTIVITIES

Advanced training is just that—advanced. Your dog must have a good foundation in basic obedience skills in order to participate. Beyond that, you can choose to get involved in just about any canine activity that appeals to you and suits your dog. Your poodle is marvelously versatile, and he is usually game to try any new activity that allows him to spend time with you.

SHOWING YOUR POODLE

Your poodle must have the correct physical attributes to be suited to the sport of Conformation shows. If your dog is well bred and possesses a strong similarity to the ideal poodle outlined in the poodle breed standard, he is a good candidate for strutting his stuff in the show ring. If he also possesses a "show off" attitude, you may just have a future champion on your hands!

Showing a dog in Conformation competition isn't quite as simple as it looks. Both you and your dog will require training. You need to learn how to handle your dog, how to hold the leash, how to present yourself, and how to dress, among many other things. Your dog has to learn how to stand for examination, how to focus on you and ignore distractions, and how to walk and trot smoothly.

The best way for both of you to learn these skills is to take a Conformation training class at a local training facility or through your local poodle club. And the best way to practice your skills is by entering a local "fun show," which is a dog show that doesn't award points toward a championship. Local clubs or businesses often sponsor these "practice" events, which provide an excellent training ground for novices.

FAST FACT

Not sure you want to participate in a canine activity? Attend several shows, competitions, training sessions, or demonstrations to get a better idea if a particular activity is a good fit for you and your dog.

OBEDIENCE

A well-trained dog is a great source of pride to his owner. Obedience is a worthy sport that will reward you and your dog for each level of Obedience you achieve. Such incentives provide plenty of motivation to advance to higher levels. Your poodle has all the qualities it takes to succeed in this sport. His intelligence makes him easy to train and his strong will to please can give you an edge over the competition.

The AKC divides Obedience competition into three levels that are successively more difficult. The Novice level requires basic Obedience skills, the Open level demands a little more discipline in basic Obedience and adds off-leash skills, and the Utility level requires the most advanced skills, including jumping, retrieving, and scent work.

To get started in Obedience, you should enroll in an Obedience training

Not sure you are ready for the "big league" of dog shows? Many local organizations have "fun shows" in which amateurs can take part.

class. Many dog-training facilities also provide practice sessions for those who have completed Obedience classes but still need to refresh their skills occasionally.

AGILITY

Perhaps the slow pace of a show ring or Obedience trial doesn't excite you. Maybe you and your poodle are both adrenaline junkies and need something more physically demanding. In that case, consider Agility, which is a wonderful dog sport that can exercise your poodle's mind as well as his body. This is a challenging sport that combines an obstacle course with the discipline of Obedience. Your smart, athletic poodle can excel in this activity as long as you're willing to make the commitment to training him.

It does take time and practice to teach your dog all the skills he'll need to successfully complete an Agility course. He must learn to weave through poles; run through tunnels; and climb, descend, and jump over various obstacles. And he must do all this while trying to break the sound barrier, because this is a timed event!

A poodle participates in the slalom, an event in the Agility competition.

FAST FACT

The sport of Agility began in Great Britain and first appeared at the Crufts Dog Show in 1979.

This sport is particularly well suited to high-energy poodles, which welcome the opportunity to burn up some of their fuel. Their owners must also enjoy a little bit of action, because they have to run alongside their dogs to direct them through the course. This is not a sport for people who would rather have their dogs do all the work! Then again, can you think of anything more fun that can keep both you and your dog mentally and physically fit?

Like Obedience competition, the best way to get started is to take lessons at a local training facility. The time and commitment you put into this activity is repaid many times over in fun and excitement.

FLYBALL

Another fast-paced and physically challenging canine sport is Flyball. If your poodle needs an outlet for his energy and loves to fetch balls, this could be his dream job! It requires speed, agility, and a true love of playing fetch.

Flyball is a team sport that is run as a relay. Each team consists of four dogs, with each dog taking his turn to run the 51-foot (15.5-meter) course. Your dog will have to jump over four jumps to get to the ball launcher at the end of the course. Then he'll have to press a pedal on the ball launcher to release a ball, retrieve the ball, and then race back over the jumps to return the ball to you.

Flyball can be as physically demanding as Agility, and should not be considered for dogs that have physical limitations. But the sport is suitable for any size dog, as the jumps are adjusted to accommodate their different sizes, and teams are divided into size categories to keep things fair for everyone. This sport has several advantages. The required training isn't as intensive as it is for Agility, and the camaraderie of being a part of a team adds another dimension to its appeal.

You can check with local dog-training facilities to find out if Flyball classes are available, or you can visit the Web site of the North American Flyball Association (NAFA), www.flyball.org, to get a list of Flyball clubs in your area.

CANINE MUSICAL FREESTYLE AND HEELWORK TO MUSIC

Another opportunity for fun is Canine Musical Freestyle. This newer dog sport consists of music, tricks, Obedience, costumes, creativity, and a good dose of applause. Also known as "dog dancing," this sport requires a dog and his handler to execute tricks and Obedience maneuvers in a dance-type routine to music. Due to its entertainment value, competitions and demonstrations of this sport tend to attract plenty of spectators!

Heelwork to Music, a similar but less theatrical version of this sport, focuses more on Obedience skills. A dog and his handler are required to perform specific skills at each level of competition.

Your poodle has showmanship in his blood, so if you want to

FAST FACT

The first large venue for Canine Musical Freestyle and Heelwork to Music was an Obedience demonstration performed to music at the Canine Pacific Showcase in British Columbia, Canada, in 1991.

showcase his talents as a performer, either of these sports would be a great fit. The physical demands are not as great as for Agility or Flyball, but these sports do require some intellectual ability. An expert Freestyle dog may learn more than 40 different commands and hand signals, but then, your poodle is more than adequately endowed with smarts!

Canine Musical Freestyle and Heelwork to Music training classes are still rather difficult to find because these are newly emerging sports, but there are a number of books and videos available through the World Canine Freestyle Organization (WCFO) that can help you get started. The WCFO is the only organization that currently sanctions and titles dogs in Freestyle and Heelwork to Music

If your poodle has a real "hot dog" personality, perhaps he might do well as a show dog.

A TITLE FOR YOUR DOG

Most canine sports and activities allow you to earn titles for your dog. This means you can put the appropriate acronym after your pet's name to indicate his title (for example, "Puffy Poodle, OTCH"). The following titles are offered in the sport of Obedience:

CD: Companion Dog

CDX: Companion Dog Excellent

UD: Utility Dog

UDX: Utility Dog Excellent

OTCH: Obedience Trial Champion

NOC: National Obedience Champion

competitions. More information can be found on its Web site, www.worldcaninefreestyle.org.

SHOW GROOMING

If you have ever seen a show poodle in his formal attire, you already realize that you'll have to take your grooming to a much higher level if you plan to show your poodle! Poodles may have acquired their reputation as spoiled and pampered pets simply because of the incredible fuss that goes into primping them for public exhibition. If you don't have any experience in show grooming, you would be wise to hire an experienced show groomer to perform this specialized task until you can gain enough experience and confidence to do it yourself.

Poodle show clips are the fanciest hairdos in all of dogdom, and it takes the utmost skill to coif a poodle for show. In order to become an expert in canine coiffures, you'll need to master all the tricks of the trade. Besides learning how to disguise subtle faults with scissors and clippers, you'll need to become thoroughly familiar with canine hair products and how to use them to enhance your dog's coat color and texture.

Observing an expert is the best way to learn these skills. Your puppy's breeder may be willing to educate you in the fine art of poodle grooming, or she may be able to refer you to someone else who can help. You can also check with your local poodle club to see if any members may be interested in mentoring you. It might seem tempting to just leave the show grooming completely to the professionals, but this will add a considerable expense to showing

Poodle Styles Grooming Chart

(Above) A poodle sporting the Continental clip. (Right) This chart shows several clipping styles, including the Miami clip (1), Retriever clip (2), Continental clip (3), Jacket and Pants clip (4), Bell Bottom clip (5), and the Puppy clip (6). There are more than two dozen possible poodle clips.

your dog. Most novices eventually work their way into grooming their own show dogs.

Retaining the services of a professional groomer doesn't relieve you of all grooming responsibilities. You must maintain your dog's coat in excellent condition between shows, because there is a limit to what a professional can do with a damaged, unkempt, or poor-quality coat.

Poodles shown in AKC-sanctioned events must be clipped in one of three acceptable show clips. The Puppy clip, which involves shaving the face, feet, and base of the tail and leaving an even clip over the rest of the body, is reserved for all poodles under the age of 12 months. Dogs over the age of 12 months must be shown in either the English Saddle clip or the Continental clip. Both of these clips show off a cleanly shaved face; a thick mane covering the thoracic area; and a ball of fur, called a pompon, on each front leg.

The English Saddle clip also includes a blanket of hair left on the hindquarters, and two pompons on each rear leg. The Continental clip, by contrast, has neatly shaved hindquarters with rosettes of hair left on the point of the hips and only one pompon on each rear leg.

OTHER ACTIVITIES FOR YOUR POODLE

There is no activity you can do with your dog that is more worthwhile than volunteer work. Because of their intelligence, poodles have proven to be excellent at providing humans assistance in a variety of ways. Two areas in which your poodle could excel include search and rescue or as a therapy dog.

SEARCH AND RESCUE: Perhaps the most honorable volunteer job for dogs is search and rescue. The rewards of reuniting parents with their lost child or giving comfort to survivors of a tragedy are incalculable. Although this work is too demanding for Toy and Miniature Poodles, the Standard Poodle's size and hunting inclinations make him a good candidate for this type of work.

A considerable commitment of time, training, and monetary expenses is required, as search-and-rescue dogs must participate in regular, intensive training sessions to become certified, and their owners are often required to cover their own expenses for travel and equipment. This activity is best for people who do not have a lot of other major commitments in life.

In addition, it takes a certain amount of fortitude to do this type of work. Disasters and tragedies can be ugly, and a search does not always result in a pleasant outcome. If you think you and your dog have what it takes to do this important and demanding job, learn more about it by visiting the Web site for the National Association for Search and Rescue (NASAR), www.nasar.org.

THERAPY DOG: A volunteer opportunity that doesn't require quite as large a commitment is therapy dog work. The benefits to humans of canine companionship have been well documented. These include lowering blood pressure, reducing stress, and even accelerating recuperation after surgery. These benefits have inspired dog owners to volunteer the companionship of their dogs for the benefit of nursing home residents, hospital patients, prison inmates, and schoolchildren.

Poodles appear to be ideally designed for this type of work. Their clean, nonshed coats are particularly welcome in health care and educational institutions, and their emotionally perceptive, outgoing, and friendly personalities make them ideal therapy dog prospects. Poodles love to be loved, and better than that, they don't mind spreading that love around.

By sharing your dog's unconditional love with others, you can bring smiles and healing to many people. But there is more involved in this process than simply taking your dog to a facility to meet the beneficiaries of your goodwill. Most facilities will require your dog to be tested and certified by a therapy dog organization such as the Delta Society or Therapy Dogs International (TDI).

To become certified, your dog must meet certain requirements that prove his suitability for therapy dog work. Not all poodles are therapy dog material. Aggressive dogs, overly excitable dogs, and dogs that have not learned basic obedience and good manners in public will not pass the certification test.

Not all dog owners are cut out for this work, either. Just because the commitment is not as consuming as it is for search-and-rescue work doesn't mean there is no commitment at all. The recipients of your therapy dog work will look forward to regular, consistent visits, usually on a weekly basis.

For more information on therapy dog testing or certification, visit the Web site for the Delta Society, www.deltasociety.org, or Therapy Dogs International, www.tdi-dog.org. These organizations can also put you in touch with local therapy dog groups that provide support for newcomers to this activity.

FAST FACT

Human companions keep finding new ways for therapy dogs to be of service. One of the newest jobs for therapy dogs is as reading partners for children. Children can read to therapy dogs without fear of judgment or criticism, thereby making reading a fun learning experience. These dogs enjoy visiting schools and public libraries.

AKC CANINE GOOD CITIZEN

Whether or not you have enough time for competitive or volunteer activities, there is one advanced training goal that every dog owner should consider. The AKC Canine Good Citizen (CGC) program promotes responsible dog ownership by awarding the CGC designation to dogs that pass its 10-step test. The test is designed to evaluate a dog's manners by showing that the dog is capable of greeting a friendly stranger, sitting politely for petting, and obeying basic Obedience commands, among other skills. The test also assesses how responsible the dog owner is by noting how well the dog is cared for, handled, and groomed.

The advantages of a CGC designation go beyond the proof that your dog is indeed a good member of society. CGC dogs may be allowed in facilities and business establishments, such as hotels, that otherwise prohibit dogs. Training and testing are offered at many dog-training facilities. The AKC Web site, www.akc.org, provides a listing of registered evaluators.

&a &a &a

Regardless of the goals you have for your adult poodle, your dog may well have his own goals in mind. He may inspire you with his zest for physical activity and convince you to pursue one of the more physically demanding canine sports, like Agility or Flyball. He may impress you with his unique sense of doggy wit and his ability to attract your attention and make you laugh, making it obvious that his true calling is doing tricks for treats or Canine Musical Freestyle. He may thrive on the challenge of search-and-rescue work. Maybe he'll make it perfectly clear that all he really wants to do is love and be loved, persuading you to share him with others through therapy dog work. You can "ask" your dog to do whatever you want, but don't be surprised if your poodle "talks" you into something else! Whatever activity you and your dog decide to pursue, there is no greater joy than being a partner with your dog.

CHAPTER EIGHT

Caring for Your Senior Poodle

As your poodle ages, you might begin to wonder if he has discovered the fountain of youth. Poodles tend to maintain their youthful appearance and behavior well into their senior years, perhaps as a result of their positive attitudes, their zest for life, or, in the case of Toy and Miniature Poodles, their longer-than-average life spans. A 10-year-old poodle might still act like a rambunctious pup, bouncing in excitement to see you, incessantly begging you to play, and spinning in circles at the

---

As your poodle ages, it is normal for him to have less energy.

prospect of going for a walk. Yet poodles do get older, and they undergo subtle changes as they age.

HEALTH PROBLEMS RELATED TO AGING

Your aging poodle may eventually show signs of joint stiffness, and his sense of hearing and vision may diminish. The incidence of ear infections, weight loss, weight gain, tumors, and dental problems increase with age, as do problems with internal processes like circulation, digestion, and organ function.

Many of these physiological changes can be addressed with proper veterinary care, so it's even more critical at this stage to maintain regular annual veterinary checkups for your poodle. Your dog does not necessarily have to suffer from maladies that appear to be unavoidable symptoms of old age.

ARTHRITIS: Arthritis, a very common ailment in older dogs, can be managed with supplements, moderate exercise, and various products that help relieve or minimize inflammation and pain. If your older poodle begins to have difficulty getting up, lying down, or jumping up on the furniture, or if he shows pain or stiffness when moving around, he may be suffering from arthritis.

If your poodle has a hard time getting up, talk to your veterinarian. There are many vitamins and supplements available to combat and relieve the pain caused by arthritis.

Supplements containing glucosamine and chondroitin can help keep his joints lubricated and flexible. In severe cases, your veterinarian may prescribe pain relievers to keep your arthritic dog comfortable.

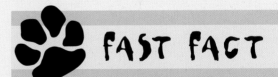

FAST FACT

Due to better diets, better living conditions, and advances in veterinary medicine, dogs are living longer than ever. Pet-product manufacturers are paying attention to the aging pet population. Supplements, special diets, low-calorie treats, and an abundance of health products and comfort devices for aging pets are now widely available at pet supply outlets.

There are dozens of products currently available to assist arthritic dogs, including orthopedic beds, electric blankets, and ramps.

WEIGHT GAIN OR LOSS: Weight gain is another common problem among older dogs. As your dog ages, his activity level decreases and his metabolism slows, which decreases his calorie needs. The problem is that these changes occur so gradually that you may not notice

FAST FACT

You can't always prevent or cure age-related conditions, but you can improve your poodle's quality of life by keeping him as comfortable as possible. Don't forget to investigate alternative therapies, such as acupuncture, chiropractic, herbal remedies, homeopathic remedies, aromatherapy, Tellington Touch, massage, or other health options.

that your dog has begun to gain weight until he already looks like an overstuffed sausage.

Keep a close eye on your dog's weight as he ages, and adjust his food consumption accordingly. If you find it too difficult to keep his weight under control by providing moderate exercise and cutting back on dog food and treats, you might consider feeding him a reduced-calorie diet. This should be done only on the advice of your veterinarian after an exam has ruled out health issues as possible causes for your dog's condition.

Your veterinarian should also be consulted if your aging dog loses weight. Weight loss can be a symptom of a more serious underlying problem, but sometimes a decrease in the sense of taste in an older dog can cause a reduction in appetite. This can be remedied by switching to

Although your pet may need some special considerations because of his age, he is still the same loyal friend he has always been, and will still want to spend lots of time with you.

FAST FACT

A dog that is 15 percent over his desirable weight is susceptible to obesity-related health problems.

a more palatable dog food to stimulate your dog's appetite.

DENTAL PROBLEMS: Dental problems become more pronounced as a dog ages, because the lifelong accumulation of tartar and plaque begins to cause problems. Toy and

Miniature Poodles are especially prone to dental problems and should have their teeth checked regularly by a veterinarian. Your vet may recommend a professional teeth cleaning, which involves anesthetizing your dog so that plaque beneath the gum line can be removed without putting your dog through any discomfort.

LOSS OF SENSES: You may notice your dog's vision beginning to wane with age, as the natural hardening of the eye lenses will sometimes cause a reduction in vision. When the lens hardens, it becomes less flexible.

A MAJOR TOOTHACHE

The accumulation of plaque and tartar under the gum line can cause a serious bacterial infection. But this infection will not be content to remain in the mouth. If left untreated, bacteria will hitch a ride through the bloodstream and settle in other parts of the body. This can make your dog quite sick.

Have your elderly dog's teeth checked regularly by your veterinarian, and keep an eye out for the following signs of dental problems:

- Red or inflamed gums
- Obvious accumulation of plaque and tartar along the gum line
- Gum recession
- Bleeding gums
- Loose teeth

- Missing teeth
- Difficulty chewing or refusal to eat
- Loss of weight
- Bad breath
- Pawing at the mouth

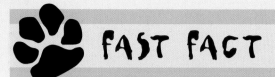

FAST FACT

Older dogs are more susceptible to the effects of temperature extremes, so don't leave your elderly poodle outside when it's extremely hot or cold, and watch your dog for signs of temperature-related distress.

This makes it more difficult for your poodle to focus. The lens can also acquire a misty appearance, like frosted glass. Poodles are incredibly adaptable and will generally adjust to this condition without assistance.

Hearing loss is also common with age and may be more pronounced in poodles that have suffered a number of serious ear infections earlier in life. If your dog becomes less responsive to your commands, you can start communicating more with hand signs and body language. You will also need to keep your dog's hearing deficiency in mind to prevent him from getting into dangerous situations.

Tumors: Older poodles are known to develop small, cauliflower-shaped skin tumors. In most cases, these are benign, but care should be taken when grooming so as not to irritate them. Softer, fleshy tumors under the skin are also common

among older dogs. These, too, are most often benign and don't need to be removed unless they are causing your dog discomfort. Even so, it is a good idea to have any type of lump checked out by your veterinarian.

A tumor that appears to grow in size, or one that becomes irritated easily and doesn't seem to heal, should be brought to your veterinarian's attention immediately. Benign tumors around the eyes, genitals, and anus are best removed to prevent them from causing further problems.

Cataracts can affect your poodle's vision.

If your poodle begins to lose his sight or hearing, his other senses will sharpen to help him get around.

CANCER: Unfortunately, not all tumors are benign. Cancer presents itself in many forms, including tumors, and can affect just about any tissue in the body. Like cancer in humans, some forms of cancer in canines are easier to treat than others or have a better chance for a good prognosis. But the treatment options for dogs are constantly expanding as cancer researchers learn more about this disease.

Although cancer isn't necessarily a terminal illness anymore, a positive outcome often depends on early detection. Symptoms of cancer may run the gamut from unusual lumps or growths to odd behaviors or physical symptoms. Anything unusual should be brought to your veterinarian's attention.

INCONTINENCE: If your older dog begins to leak urine while sleeping, or seems to have trouble "holding it" for long periods of time when you're at work, he may have a problem with incontinence. This is an extremely unpleasant condition, but there are things you can do to manage it.

First, have your dog examined by your veterinarian. Urine leakage in older dogs is sometimes caused by a relaxation of the sphincter muscle that releases urine from the bladder. This condition can sometimes be remedied with medication prescribed by your vet. If your dog is consuming a lot of water and needs to urinate frequently, he may be suffering from a reduction in kidney function. Again, your vet may be able to help you manage this condition with medication or dietary changes.

Second, you can take steps to minimize accidents and manage the problem. Be sure to take your dog outside frequently for potty breaks, and provide your dog with a washable bed that can be cleaned whenever necessary. You can find cummerbunds (for males) and britches (for females) in some pet supply stores and pet catalogs. These can prevent urine from dribbling around the house and make it much easier to live with an incontinent dog.

FAILING ORGANS: Your senior dog may also experience a reduction in some organ function. The liver and kidneys do not always function as efficiently in old age as they did when your poodle was young. Your dog may develop a sensitive stomach or he may suffer from some degree of heart failure. Watch for symptoms like excessive water consumption (signaling liver or kidney problems); refusal to eat, vomiting, or diarrhea (stomach or digestive problems); and lack of energy, difficulty breathing during exertion, or water retention (heart problems).

It is wise to seek the advice of a veterinarian regarding any unusual symptoms or behavior in your aging poodle. The underlying cause of any symptom must be determined before treatment or management options can be discussed. With the proper veterinary care, you can improve the quality of your poodle's life and greatly extend his life span.

NUTRITION

The face of commercial dog food has changed dramatically over the last couple decades, with more canine diet options now available than ever before. Among these options are specialty diets that can help address various canine health conditions. For example, a diet low in phosphorous is available for dogs suffering from kidney problems. A diet low in carbohydrates can help manage canine diabetes mellitus. A diet devoid of salt can alleviate heart problems. A diet low in calories can help treat obesity. There are even commercial diets formulated especially for dogs with sensitive stomachs or food allergies.

If your dog suffers from any age-related condition, it doesn't hurt to investigate specialty diets as a possible treatment. Most of these diets must be prescribed by and purchased from a veterinarian. Your veterinarian may also be able to recommend certain vitamins and supplements to help manage conditions associated with old age.

In the absence of any health issues, your senior dog will do just fine on an adult maintenance version of dog food, provided his weight and the amount fed to him are monitored. If dental problems are an issue—if he has lost some teeth, for example—you may need to consider offering your older dog softer foods (canned, or dry food mixed with water) or smaller, easier-to-chew kibble.

EXERCISE

How much exercise does your older poodle need? What's too little exercise, or too much? There really isn't a fine line between too much exercise and too little exercise for an older poodle. There's a huge range in the middle that can be explored, depending on your dog's normal energy level, health condition, and fitness. There are just two things you need to do: provide exercise on a regular

basis, and watch for signs of overexertion.

Moderate, regular exercise is a great way to maintain your dog's good health, and helps manage obesity, arthritis, and digestive or heart

Your elderly poodle will still need exercise and will always love to play. Just be sure that the exercise is appropriate for his age and condition, and that he doesn't overexert himself.

problems in the older dog. But you should avoid overworking your senior poodle. Signs of overexertion or heat exhaustion include panting in excess of five or ten minutes after exercise, collapse, and elevated temperature. Arthritic dogs will show increased stiffness if they are exercised too much or too little.

Your elderly poodle will appreciate the fresh air of a daily walk and a fun game of fetch once a day. Life doesn't have to become boring in old age. Your aged poodle will still want to be included in everything you do and experience new things once in a while. In addition to physical activities, keep your poodle's mind sharp through mental exercise. Albert Einstein didn't stop being a genius in old age, and your poodle, likewise, doesn't lose IQ points as he matures.

SAYING GOOD-BYE

It is a sad fact that dogs are not allowed as much time on this earth as humans, so the day will eventually come when you will have to part with your cherished poodle. When a poodle has woven his way tightly into the fabric of your life, it can be incredibly difficult to break such strong threads.

Even though we hope for a peaceful death for our canine friends, death is rarely so idyllic in real life.

In most cases, death is a slow, cruel process that involves a failing body and lingering pain. In order to ease your pet's suffering at the end of his life, you may have to make the decision to euthanize him.

EUTHANASIA

This is one of the most difficult decisions you will have to make as a pet owner, but also one of the kindest things you can do for your canine companion. If you "listen" to your dog, he will probably help make the decision for you. He will tell you that he is very tired and ready for eternal rest. It may be through the look in his eyes, the subdued wag of his tail, or his refusal to get up or eat. You will know when the time is right.

Euthanasia is a term that means "good death," and there really is no better way to describe it. Your veterinarian will inject a mixture of drugs into your dog's vein that will cause him to fall asleep immediately. A few moments later, your dog's life will gently stop when his heart stops beating.

Your veterinarian will ask you how you would like to dispose of your dog's remains. This should be your decision alone—don't worry about what others think. If you want to have your dog cremated and keep his ashes in an urn, if you want to bury your dog in a pet cemetery so you can mark the grave, or if you want to leave this responsibility entirely in the hands of your veterinarian, you should make whatever arrangements make you feel the most comfortable. How you handle your dog's cremation or burial can help you cope with your grief.

COPING WITH GRIEF

Losing a canine partner can be devastating. Even if you attempt to mentally prepare for the loss in advance, you may be surprised by the overwhelming feelings of grief and sadness. Here are some suggestions that may help:

MEMORIALIZE YOUR DOG: A memorial can be anything that will allow you to remember your poodle in a positive way. You can plant a tree, frame a photo of your dog, construct your own grave marker, or post a memorial on one of dozens of

Making a memorial stone for your poodle may help the grieving process.

Remember the good times with your poodle by looking at some old photographs, or perhaps assemble an album of your favorites to review when you're feeling down.

Internet sites that feature pet memorials. You can also make a charitable donation in your dog's name to an organization that is working to improve the health, quality of life, and longevity of dogs, such as a canine health foundation, a veterinary college, or a poodle rescue organization. Another worthy recipient might be your veterinarian. He could use the money toward a new piece of equipment that would help him to care for other dogs, or you could earmark your donation to go toward care for dogs with indigent owners.

REDIRECT YOUR FOCUS: It takes time to get over the pain of such a difficult loss, but it won't make you feel any better to dwell on your poodle's death. Keeping busy is a great way to occupy your mind with something else. Start a project, take up a new hobby, or plan a trip. You could use something to look forward to right now, and any type of new activity can help fill the void left by your dear departed poodle.

You might be tempted to fill this painful void by getting a new pet, but this is only a good idea if you feel absolutely ready for it. A better idea is to focus on the people and other pets that are already in your life. By spreading your love a little thicker on those close to you, the wonderfully elastic quality of love will stretch over the aching hole in your heart. Then, after the pain has faded, you might find yourself searching classified ads or breeders' listings for—you guessed it—another poodle!

⩘ ⩘ ⩘

By keeping your poodle happy and healthy during the twilight of his life, you'll be able to collect many more wonderful memories of your life together. In the end, you'll realize how truly rich your own life has been in the company of your curly friend. You'll savor adventure, excitement, fun, happiness, and also a few challenges when you share your life with a poodle. Would you deny yourself any of it?

Organizations to Contact

**American Animal
Hospital Association**
12575 West Bayaud Ave.
Lakewood, CO 80228
Phone: 303-986-2800
Fax: 800-252-2242
Email: info@aahanet.org
Web site: www.aahanet.org

American Kennel Club
260 Madison Ave
New York, NY 10016
Phone: 212-696-8200
Web site: www.akc.org

Association of Pet Dog Trainers
150 Executive Center Drive, Box 35
Greenville, SC 29615
Phone: 1-800-738-3647
Fax: 1-864-331-0767
Email: information@apdt.com
Web site: www.apdt.com

The Canadian Kennel Club
89 Skyway Avenue, Suite 100
Etobicoke, Ontario
M9W 6R4 Canada
Phone: 416-675-5511
Fax: 416-675-6506
Email: information@ckc.ca
Web site: www.ckc.ca/en/

**Canine Eye Registration
Foundation**
1717 Philo Road
P.O. Box 3007
Urbana, IL 61803-3007
Phone: 217-693-4800
Fax: 217-693-4801
Email: cerf@vmdb.org
Web site: www.vmdb.org/cerf.html

Delta Society
875 124th Avenue NE, Suite 101
Bellevue, WA 98005
Phone: 425-226-7357
Fax: 425-679-5539
Email: info@deltasociety.org
Web site: www.deltasociety.org

**The Kennel Club
of the United Kingdom**
1-5 Clarges Street
Piccadilly
London W1J 8AB
United Kingdom
Phone: 0870 606 6750
Fax: 020 7518 1058
Web site: www.thekennelclub.org.uk/

The Miniature Poodle Club
Milburn, Langtoft
PE6 9LE
United Kingdom
Phone: 01778-348106
Fax: same as phone
Email: Jackie@
        michandypoodles.co.uk
Web site:
        www.miniaturepoodleclub.org.uk

National Association of Dog Obedience Instructors
PMB 369
729 Grapevine Hwy
Hurst, TX 76054-2085
Email: corrsec2@nadoi.org
Web site: www.nadoi.org

National Association of Professional Pet Sitters
17000 Commerce Parkway, Suite C
Mt. Laurel, NJ 08054
Phone: 856-439-0324
Fax: 856-439-0525
Email: napps@ahint.com
Web site: www.petsitters.org

North American Dog Agility Council (NADAC)
11522 South Highway 3
Cataldo, ID 83810
Email: info@nadac.com
Web site: www.nadac.com

North American Flyball Association (NAFA)
1400 West Devon Avenue, #512
Chicago, IL 60660
Phone: 800-318-6312
Fax: same as phone
Email: flyball@flyball.org
Web site: www.flyball.org

Pet Sitters International
418 East King Street
King, NC 27021-9163
Phone: 336-983-9222
Fax: 336-983-3755
Web site: www.petsit.com

Poodle Club of America, Inc.
2434 Ripplewood Drive
Conroe, TX 77384
Phone: 936-271-0397
Email: infopoodleclubofamerica@
        yahoo.com
Web site:
        www.poodleclubofamerica.org

Poodle Club of Canada
46 Main Street
Hillsburgh, Ontario N0B 1Z0
Canada
Phone: 519-855-4903
Email: denalipoodles@sympatico.ca
Web site:
        www.poodleclubcanada.com

Teacup Dogs Agility Association (TDAA)
P.O. Box 158
Maroa, IL 61756
Phone: 217-521-7955
Email: agilitygo1@msn.com
Web site: www.k9tdaa.com

Therapy Dogs International, Inc.
88 Bartley Road
Flanders, NJ 07836
Phone: 973-252-9800
Fax: 973-252-7171
Email: tdi@gti.net
Web site: www.tdi-dog.org

UK National Pet Register
74 North Albert Street, Dept 2
Fleetwood, Lancashire
FY7 6BJ
United Kingdom
Web site: www.nationalpetregister.org

United States Dog Agility Association, Inc. (USDAA)
P.O. Box 850955
Richardson, TX 75085-0955
Phone: 972-487-2200
Fax: 972-272-4404
Email: info@usdaa.com
Web site: www.usdaa.com

World Canine Freestyle Organization (WCFO)
P.O. Box 350122
Brooklyn, NY 11235-2525
Phone: 718-332-8336
Fax: 718-646-2686
Email: wcfodogs@aol.com
Web site:
www.worldcaninefreestyle.org

Further Reading

Arden, Darlene. *Small Dogs, Big Hearts: A Guide to Caring for Your Little Dog*, rev. ed. New York: Howell Book House, 2006.

Biniok, Janice. *The Toy and Miniature Poodle*. Neptune City, N.J.: TFH Publications, 2006.

Budiansky, Stephen. *The Truth About Dogs: An Inquiry into the Ancestry, Social Conventions, Mental Habits, and Moral Fiber of Canis Familiaris*. New York: Viking, 2000.

Coren, Stanley. *The Intelligence of Dogs: Canine Consciousness and Capabilities*. New York: The Free Press, 1994.

Geeson, Eileen. *The Complete Standard Poodle*. New York: Howell Book House, 1998.

John, Meredith, and Carole L. Richards. *Raising a Champion: A Beginner's Guide to Showing Dogs*. Collingswood, N.J.: The Well Trained Dog, 2001.

Kalstone, Shirlee. *Poodle Clipping and Grooming: The International Reference*. New York: Howell Book House, 2000.

Tortora, Daniel F. *The Right Dog for You*. New York: Simon and Schuster, 1980.

Wood, Deborah. *Little Dogs: Training Your Pint-Sized Companion*. Neptune City, N.J.: TFH Publications, 2004.

Internet Resources

www.akc.org/breeds/poodle/

This page contains the American Kennel Club's description of the poodle breed standard.

www.aspca.org/apcc

The ASPCA Animal Poison Control Center provides lifesaving information for pet owners. The center also has a hot line available for emergencies: 888-426-4435

www.avma.org

The American Veterinary Medical Association Web site provides a wealth of information on canine health and welfare issues for pet owners.

www.canismajor.com/dog/

This Web site has a tremendous library of articles about dogs, covering everything from hereditary health issues to breed profiles. Have a question about dogs? You can look it up here.

www.ckc.ca/en/Default.aspx?tabid=99&BreedCode=POL

This page contains the Canadian Kennel Club's description of the poodle breed standard.

www.petfinder.com

A nationwide database of adoptable pets, which also provides listings of shelters and poodle rescue groups.

www.petrix.com/dognames/

Can't think of a catchy name for your poodle? This Web site will give you all kinds of ideas, from traditional to strangely unique!

www.petsitters.org

The Web site of the National Association of Professional Pet Sitters can be used to help poodle owners locate a professional pet sitter in their area.

www.poodlehistory.org

Interesting collection of historical documents and information pertaining to poodles.

www.thekennelclub.org.uk/item/169

This page contains the Kennel Club of the United Kingdom's description of the poodle breed standard.

www.upei.ca/cidd/intro.htm

University of Prince Edward Island in Canada provides this wonderful document on the hereditary disorders of dogs. Look up the poodle breed to get in-depth information on virtually all the disorders that affect poodles.

Index

Contributors

JANICE BINIOK has written numerous articles and several books on companion animals including *The Toy and Miniature Poodle* (TFH Publications, 2006). She has an English degree from the University of Wisconsin–Milwaukee and is a member of the Dog Writers Association of America. Janice is a former professional dog groomer, and poodles have been some of her best friends and clients. Janice lives on a small farm in Waukesha, Wisconsin, with her husband, two sons, and several four-legged members of the family.

Senior Consulting Editor **GARY KORSGAARD, DVM,** has had a long and distinguished career in veterinary medicine. After graduating from The Ohio State University's College of Veterinary Medicine in 1963, he spent two years as a captain in the Veterinary Corps of the U.S. Army. During that time he attended the Walter Reed Army Institute of Research and became Chief of the Veterinary Division for the Sixth Army Medical Laboratory at the Presidio, San Francisco.

In 1968 Dr. Korsgaard founded the Monte Vista Veterinary Hospital in Concord, California, where he practiced for 32 years as a small animal veterinarian. He is a past president of the Contra Costa Veterinary Association, and was one of the founding members of the Contra Costa Veterinary Emergency Clinic, serving as president and board member of that hospital for nearly 30 years.

Dr. Korsgaard retired in 2000, and currently enjoys golf, hiking, international travel, and spending time with his wife Susan and their three children and four grandchildren.